STYLE AND DISCOURSE

With special reference to the text of
the Greek New Testament

E A Nida
J P Louw
A H Snyman
J v W Cronje

BIBLE SOCIETY

STYLE AND DISCOURSE

With special reference to the text of
the Greek New Testament

First Edition 1983

© BSSA 1983

Published by the Bible Society,
P.O. Box 6215, Roggebaai, Cape Town 8012

Printed by N.B.P.,
Goodwood, Cape

BSSA — 2½ M — 1983

ISBN 0 7982 0603 9

C O N T E N T S

C O N T E N T S

P R E F A C E

In January 1982 a group of Greek and New Testament Scholars[1] met at the University of Pretoria under the auspices of the Department of Greek and of the Institute for Interlingual Communication of the South African Bible Society.

During a series of 38 seminars on various aspects of style and discourse, both in terms of general literary theory and of significant features of ancient and modern languages, special attention was focused on stylistic formations and their function in the discourse structure of the Greek New Testament.

The resultant material from these seminars were then taken further by the authors of this volume spending a fortnight at the University of the Orange Free State in Bloemfontein selecting, arranging and reworking various opinions and relevant views arrived at during the seminars in Pretoria to

---

1) Dr E A Nida (retired Translations Research Coordinator of the United Bible Societies and Translations Secretary of the American Bible Society), Prof J H Barkhuizen (University of Pretoria), Dr J v W Cronjé (University of the Orange Free State), Prof H L F Drijepondt (University of the Orange Free State), Prof P J du Plessis (Randse Afrikaanse University), Prof A B du Toit (University of Pretoria), Prof E R Harty (University of South Africa), Prof B C Lategan (University of Stellenbosch), Mr L V le Roux (University of the Orange Free State), Prof J P Louw (University of Pretoria), Prof H Ohlhoff (University of Pretoria), Prof G M M Pelser (University of Pretoria), Mr S J P Riekert (University of the Orange Free State), Prof J H Roberts (University of South Africa), Prof A H Snyman (University of the Orange Free State), Mr H F Stander (University of Pretoria), Mr G J Swart (University of Pretoria), Mr J C Thom (University of Stellenbosch), Prof W C v Wyk (University of Pretoria), Prof W S Vorster (University of South Africa), Dr E Wendland (Translations Consultant, Zambian Bible Society), Ds J L P Wolmarans (Randse Afrikaanse University).

draft a detailed outline of the chapters and subsections of the present volume.

Thereafter, Eugene Nida wrote the basic text of this book which was then reviewed by the collaborators and finally edited by Nida with the assistance of Jannie Louw.

This book is intended, not only as a treatise on style and discourse with emphasis on the Greek New Testament but also, and perhaps especially so, as a tool for Bible translators calling for a full acceptance of the necessity to acknowledge the significance of style as an imperative component in any theory and practice of translation.

The South African Bible Society under the leadership of Gerrit van der Merwe sponsored the research and publishing of this book as the first in a series of basic tools planned to further the work of the Society's translation programs.

Special recognition is due to Stienie Venter for ably preparing the typescript and to Andries Snyman and Willem Oliver for proofreading of the final text.

J P Louw

CHAPTER 1

Rhetorical Signs

Does the Greek phrase κατὰ τὴν ἐνέργειαν τοῦ κράτους τῆς ἰσχύος αὐτοῦ (literally 'unto the power of the strength of his might') in Ephesians 1.19 really refer to three different forms of power, or is this simply a rhetorical device for piling up close synonyms as a means of emphasizing the 'immeasurable greatness of his power?' Or in Luke 1.47, do the Greek terms ψυχή and πνεῦμα (often translated 'soul' and 'spirit', respectively) refer to distinct aspects or parts of personality, or does the parallelism of the corresponding lines suggest that this is simply two different ways of speaking about human personality in 'my soul magnifies the Lord and my spirit rejoices in God my Savior?' Or in Matthew 7.6, is one to understand the action of the pigs as trampling the pearls under foot and then turning to attack, or is it simply that the pigs trample the pearls under foot and the dogs turn and attack? In other words, is one to recognize in Matthew 7.6 a type of chiastic structure, so that the meaningful relationship between the four clauses is actually a b b a, in which the first and fourth clauses refer to the dogs and the second and third clauses refer to the pigs?

To attempt to answer these questions and many more which are far more complex, it is essential to recognize that the meaning of a text is signalled by a number of different features including sounds, words, grammatical constructions, and rhetorical devices. Even what is talked about may in turn serve as a symbol for a further projected meaning. For example, the fact that people cast branches in the path of Jesus as he rode into Jerusalem meant that they were honoring him; but in various parts of Africa, to do this would have almost the opposite meaning, for it would be a sign of disrespect and of overt rejection.

As a means of understanding better how various features of a discourse may have meaning by pointing beyond themselves to something else, it is important to look to semiotics, the science of signs. The basic relationships in semiotics are not, however, a straight line between a sign and its referent, but a triadic relationship involving a sign, a referent, and the system of signs which makes possible that identification of a particular sign with its referent. In the case of the red light of traffic signs, the meaning of 'stop' depends upon the fact that there are three different colors, red, green, and yellow. It is the contrast between these colors which provides the system for a relatively arbitrary assignment of meaning.[1]

Some of the most commonly known types of signs include (1) natural signs, for example, wet streets as a sign of rain (or possibly, street cleaning), a rainbow as a sign of a passing shower; (2) artifacts such as road signs with designs identifying lodging, food, and fuel; (3) gestures, for example, pointing with the index finger, raising the hands in surrender; and (4) verbal signs, which so often depend for their meaning upon highly structured semantic domains of signs having related meanings. This is particularly true of verbal kinship terms such as <u>father</u>, <u>mother</u>, <u>son</u>, <u>daughter</u>, <u>brother</u>, <u>sister</u>, <u>uncle</u>, <u>aunt</u>, etc.[2]

A system of signs may be very limited, as in the case of

---

1   For a helpful introduction to semiotics in relation to the domains of meaning, see Eugene A. Nida, 1982, <u>Signs, Sense, and Translation</u> (Pretoria, South Africa: Pretoria University, Department of Greek). See also the last part of Chapter 10, in which some of the semiotic aspects of texts are treated.

2   For a treatment of semantic domains, see Adrienne Lehrer, 1974, <u>Semantic Fields and Lexical Structure</u> (Amsterdam, London: North-Holland Publishing Company) and Eugene A. Nida, 1975, <u>Componential Analysis of Meaning</u> (The Hague: Mouton Publishers).

red, green, and yellow lights, or it may be extremely complex as, for example, in the hundreds of words in English
dealing with communication, but in all instances a sign has
its meaning only by virtue of its relationship to other
signs with which it shares certain features (that is to say,
exhibits some similarity), and with which it contrasts. The
extent to which certain features of such signs are similar
or contrastive determines the semantic distance between
them.

The semiotic relationship between signs, referents, and the
related systems of signs quite obviously cannot exist apart
from particular interpreters, that is to say, organisms that
recognize these relationships, and in human beings these relationships are normally passed on as a part of the culture.[3]

In addition to an interpreter one must also be concerned in
communication with various types of settings. These are
normally textual, communicative, and cultural. The textual
setting may be particularly important in reinforcing
meaning. For example, in Luke 15 the significance of the
story of the prodigal son is certainly heightened by the
fact that the two preceding parables, namely, those concerning the lost sheep and the lost coin, set the stage for
the theological significance of the story of the prodigal
son, since the focus of the two previous parables is the celebration in heaven over one who repents.

---

3   It is essential to avoid the confusion between an orga-
nism which functions as an interpreter of a sign and
the term "interpretant" used by Charles Peirce, a term
which he used primarily to designate a formulation
based on the system of signs which makes possible the
relationship between a particular sign and its corresponding referent. For Peirce it was simply the system
of signs, particularly in the case of language, which
provides the means for the understanding of any one
sign.

The communicative setting is also important in understanding the significance of a discourse. Also in Luke 15 the fact that the parables are directed primarily to the Pharisees and the teachers of the law is highly significant, for these were the very persons who were complaining that Jesus was associating with outcasts and even dining with them. The communicative setting, therefore, highlights the role of the older brother in the third parable.

The cultural setting may also be extremely important for a discourse. In the case of the parable of the lost coin, the drachma would not only be an equivalent of a day's wage and thus represent considerable buying power, but it was probably a part of the headdress of a wedding costume and therefore something that would have great sentimental value for the woman who searched so thoroughly to find it and rejoiced so much when she finally recovered it.

It is normally not difficult to recognize the referent of a verbal symbol, that is, the object or event to which a word refers. What is more complex is to determine the referent of an arrangement of verbal signs, not in the sense of a syntactic construction but in terms of a rhetorical ordering. In the case of the beatitudes in Matthew 5.3-10, the occurence of μακάριοι 'happy' (or possibly 'truly fortunate') at the beginning of each beatitude rather than in a predicate position certainly highlights the paradoxical meaning of the beatitudes. Note how flat the beatitudes would be if they were rendered as

> 'Those who show mercy are happy
> because they will be shown mercy.'

or

> 'Those whose hearts are pure are happy
> because they will see God.'

The additional fact that all of the beatitudes have a parallel structure also reinforces the significance of the rhetorical order of words. This parallelism signals not only the importance of the initial word μακάριοι 'happy', but it also serves to indicate that the various beatitudes belong together and have a unity of both structure and content. At the same time, however, there is a fascinating contrast. In verses 3 and 10 the tense is present, 'for theirs is the kingdom of heaven', while in verses 4-9 the tenses are all future. Accordingly, the imminence of the kingdom of heaven is highlighted in contrast with the significant blessings which follow.

In addition to the meaningful arrangements of verbal signs, one must also reckon with the selection of particular linguistic forms. The fact that so many of the second lines in the beatitudes are in the passive form is itself significant. Such passives clearly reflect the so-called "avoidance of the divine agency". One should not, therefore, interpret such passives as meaning some kind of automatic result which is to take place. These passives are a typical case of positive taboo in avoiding naming God as the agent. Accordingly, a more explicit translation of verses 6 and 7 would be

'Happy are those who hunger and thirst to do what is right
    because God will satisfy them fully.
  Happy are those who are merciful to others
    for God will be merciful to them.'

The rendering of verse 9 is particularly significant, since shifting from a passive to an active form in the second line gives the rendering

'Happy are those who work for peace
    for God will call them his children.'

Such a rendering certainly accords with experience, for those who seek peace are often the object of severe criticism, misunderstanding, and even open hostility by those on both sides of a conflict. So often it is only God who recognizes them as his children.

The use of figurative language may in itself be a significant semiotic device. For example, in Luke 1.68-79 (the prophecy of Zechariah) such phrases as 'horn of salvation', 'house of David', 'through the mouth of his holy prophets', 'bowels of mercy', 'shadow of death', and 'way of peace' immediately signal the poetic nature of the discourse and suggest its close relationship to the Psalms, though it is not a quotation of passages in the Psalms but a kind of pastiche of typical biblical expressions used in worship.

The use of rhetorical questions may be particularly effective, for though they have a form of questions, they are usually equivalent to emphatic declarations. Furthermore, as rhetorical questions they assume that the audience will be fully cognizant of the implications of such questions. Accordingly, a speaker or writer may thus identify with his audience by implying that the audience will obviously agree. The series of such rhetorical questions in Romans 8.31-35 is particularly effective, for example, 'In view of this, what then shall we say?' 'If God is for us, who can be against us?' 'The one who did not spare his own son, but gave him up on behalf of all of us, how is it possible that he would not together with him give us all things?' 'Who will bring accusations against those whom God has chosen?' In some languages, however, one cannot use a rhetorical question without immediately providing an answer, and in other languages rhetorical questions are simply not used. Equivalent expressions would be strong, positive declarations.

Some persons have been so impressed with what they regard as the unique character of the Greek New Testament that they assume that the writers of the New Testament invented the various rhetorical devices. On the other hand, others have assumed that the writers must have used such expressions as purely a matter of chance, in other words, as strictly accidental ways of having expressed some concept. Still other persons assume that those who study the stylistic features

of the Greek New Testament have themselves invented terms to
fit ways of speaking which are simply natural for the Greek
language itself. None of these attempts to explain some of
the significant features of New Testament style are
adequate. At the same time, it is impossible to determine
the degree to which New Testament writers may have been
consciously aware of the rhetorical structures which they
employed. For one thing, rhetoric was such a fundamental
aspect of all levels of education that effective use of a
language would be almost second nature to any person with
literary training or experience.

The New Testament reflects two diverse but at the same time
complementary sources of rhetorical structure. The one reflects the Hebrew of the Old Testament, which is conspicuous in so many passages of the Septuagint translation of
Hebrew into Greek, made some 200 years before Christ. One
might even call the Greek of the Septuagint a kind of
"Semitized Greek". No doubt there was also a good deal of
what is regarded as "linguistic contamination" in the
writing of bilinguals. Many Semitic features were carried
over into the New Testament since so many underlying sources
for the New Testament reflect an oral tradition which had
undergone important Aramaic influence. [4]

The figurative language in Zechariah's prophecy (cited just
above) certainly reflects vividly the rich resources of
figurative expressions used in the Old Testament. No doubt
many instances of parallelism in the New Testament are
echoes of the abundant parallelism in the Hebrew text,
especially of the Psalms. Note the parallelism in Psalm
148.1-4, as reflected in the Revised Standard Version:

---

4   See Mathew Black, 1954, <u>An Aramaic Approach to the
     Gospels and Acts</u> (Oxford: Oxford University Press).

> Praise the LORD!
> Praise the LORD from the heavens,
>> praise him in the heights!
> Praise him, all his angels,
>> praise him, all his host!
> Praise him, sun and moon,
>> praise him, all you shining stars!
> Praise him, you highest heavens,
>> and you waters above the heavens!

In many instances, however, the parallelism is not so obvious. Note for example Psalm 89.20-23 in the Revised Standard Version:

> I have found David, my servant;
>> with my holy oil I have anointed him;
> so that my hand shall ever abide with him,
>> my arm also shall strengthen him.
> The enemy shall not outwit him,
>> the wicked shall not humble him.
> I will crush his foes before him
>> and strike down those who hate him.

In the Hebrew Old Testament there is a great deal of inverted parallelism called chiasm, and this is particularly conspicuous in certain parts of the prophetic books. In Amos 5.4-5,

> For thus says the LORD to the house of Israel:
>> "Seek me and live;
>>> but do not seek Bethel,
>> and do not enter into Gilgal
>>> or cross over to Beer-sheba;
>> for Gilgal shall surely go into exile,
>>> and Bethel shall come to nought."

The order Bethel, Gilgal, Beer-sheba, Gilgal, and Bethel reflects an a b c b a pattern, typical of chiastic stuctures of the Old Testament and of what often occurs in the New Testament.

In Hebrew there is a significant pattern of avoidance of divine names, especially the tetragrammaton YHWH which was normally not pronounced. The name of Yahweh was pointed so that the reader would pronounce the title Adonai 'Lord'. Other substitute expressions were 'the Highest' or 'the Almighty' or 'the Holy One of Israel'. Since the Septuagint translation of the Old Testament was the "Bible" of the early church, it is not at all strange that numerous rhetorical features of Hebrew found their way into the Greek of the New Testament.

A far more important source of rhetorical features in the New Testament is to be found, however, in the writings of Greek authors, which clearly reflect the dominant emphasis upon rhetoric in the educational system of the Hellenistic world. In a sense, prose rhetoric formed the mainstream of the whole of ancient education in the Hellenistic world.

A landmark in the history of speech composition was the visit of Gorgias of Leontini to Athens in 427 B.C. Rhetoric, particularly on the level of individual sentences with their balanced clauses and rhythms, constituted Gorgias's main contribution to literature. Empedocles, a pupil of Gorgias, left many examples of this type of highly elaborate and intricate stylistic manipulation. But even before the time of Gorgias, two Sicilians, Corax and Tisias, had written handbooks on public speaking, and even the philosophers who preceded Socrates evidently gave great attention to the rhetorical forms in which they expounded their ideas.[5]

---

5   For an analysis of the influence of Gorgias and the early rhetoricians, see G. Kennedy, 1963, The Art of Persuasion in Greece (Princeton: Princeton University Press).

One of the most famous schools of rhetoric in ancient Greece was that of Isocrates, another student of Gorgias. His style abounded in figures of speech, having a resemblance to poetry with its rhythmic flow. His emphasis upon repetition, parallelism, and contrast came to be greatly appreciated. The following examples from Paul clearly exhibit some of these rhetorical devices: ἵνα ἐν παντὶ πάντοτε πᾶσαν αὐτάρκειαν ἔχοντες 2 Corinthians 9.8 (literally, 'in order that having complete sufficiency always in every circumstance'); ἐν ᾧ γὰρ κρίνεις τὸν ἕτερον, σεαυτὸν κατακρίνεις Romans 2.1 (literally, 'in what you judge another, yourself you condemn'); εἰ γὰρ τῷ τοῦ ἑνὸς παραπτώματι οἱ πολλοὶ ἀπέθανον, πολλῷ μᾶλλον ἡ χάρις τοῦ θεοῦ καὶ ἡ δωρεὰ ἐν χάριτι τῇ τοῦ ἑνὸς ἀνθρώπου Ἰησοῦ Χριστοῦ εἰς τοὺς πολλοὺς ἐπερίσσευσεν Romans 5.15 (literally, 'for if by the transgression of one person, many died, by so much more the grace of God and the gift by the grace of one person Jesus Christ will abound to many'). The numerous parallels in the Greek structure of 1 Corinthians 13 are especially characteristic of the style of Isocrates.

In Plato's Academy and Aristotle's Lyceum, the most famous schools of antiquity, courses were offered in a wide variety of subjects, including mathematics, astronomy, botany, zoology, philosophy. But especially in the Hellenistic period rhetoric became one of the most important subjects of all, since it not only afforded grammatical and compositional insights into literature (and especially poetry), but was also regarded by the Greeks as the most characteristic feature of an educated person.[6] In Hellenistic times this pattern of education, begun in classical Athens, was developed into an

---

6   Plato himself was one of the most famous and thoroughgoing opponents of the rhetoric of the sophists, whose logic was so often sterile and whose interest in rhetoric seemed directed more to cleverness rather than to substantive truth.

even more definite form which endured largely until the end
of the ancient world.[7] But central to all studies in the
ancient world was the concentration on rhetoric. In fact,
it outgrew its original function of providing instruction in
persuasive speech and became what one might regard as the
principal educational instrument in the spread of Greek
thought and culture.

In many approaches to rhetoric and style a number of fundamental considerations have been lacking. In the first
place, there seems to be no comprehensive system into which
the various functions and features of rhetoric and style may
fit. Perhaps one of the reasons for this is that many
scholars have not recognized that there are more functions
than have been traditionally treated. This may be due to
the fact that no clear distinction has been made between the
macrolevel and the microlevel of rhetoric.

In many instances analyses of function in language have not
distinguished three important relations: (a) discourse to
intent, (b) discourse to the real world, and (c) discourse
to the response of receptors. But probably the most serious
failure has arisen from the fact that the signification of
these functions has not been treated in a semiotic sense.
Thinking of meaning only in terms of lexical items or propositions has often led persons to disregard the crucial
role of rhetorical features as signs having meaning for
receptors. The explication of the meaning of such signs
cannot be accomplished in the same manner as one defines
lexical meanings by componential features, but anything
which serves as a sign of something for receptors has
meaning in this broad semiotic sense. In order to grasp the

---

7   For a discussion of the development of rhetoric in the
    ancient world, see G. Kennedy, 1972, The Art of Rheto-
    ric in the Roman World (Princeton: Princeton Universi-
    ty Press).

significance of rhetorical features it is therefore preferable to classify these features in terms of processes, for the nature of the process is really the key to the semiotic significance of such features. As a means of putting the various elements of this approach to rhetoric and style in to proper perspective, it seems best to treat first the structures and then their functions.

The treatment of rhetorical features appears to be more readily comprehended if one deals first with the macrolevel and then the microlevel, but the size of units is not the primary consideration; rather, it is the relation of the parts to the whole.

The macrolevel of rhetorical structure involves primarily the broader and more inclusive units which are normally related semantically, while the rhetorical features on the microlevel generally serve to relate units on the macrolevel or to increase impact and appeal by various formal devices. The two dyadic elements on the macrolevel of rhetorical features consist of progression and cohesion, (two complementary aspects of the same rhetorical coin) which account for both the diversity and the unity of discourse.

Progression involves four basic discourse types. The first consists of a set of related events with one or more strings of participants in which the events are organized essentially in terms of temporal progression. This basic type of temporal organization of discourse elements may consist of a personal narrative about a sequence of events, a story with its typical scenario of steady state, complication, crisis, resolution, and modified state, or a set of instructions to be followed in a particular sequence. A set of events need not be treated in strictly historical order. One may begin a story in the middle and by means of back-flashes introduce necessary data concerning earlier events. One may also plant information in advance in what may be called "forward-flashes". But in the first basic type of progression the fundamental feature consists of a series of related events whether or not in strictly chronological order.

The second basic type of progression consists of what one might well call a "descriptive series". In this case objects and events are organized either spatially or in terms of categories. Spatial organizations of description depend primarily on the so-called "viewpoint character". For example, one may describe a house in terms of the various features that a viewpoint character may encounter as he moves through a house, beginning with the porch and entranceway, and then a hall, various rooms, the upstairs, possibly the cellar, and finally the back door. There is no specified series of events, but the presumed movement of the viewpoint character through space provides a basis for description. Similarly, the description of a person is often spatially organized, and this is also generally true of the description of a landscape.

On the other hand, a descriptive series may be based primarily upon a set of categories. For example, a house may be described in terms of the number of doors, windows, rooms, floors, heating vents, electrical outlets, etc. Events may also be described in terms of types of features rather than series of related episodes. In many instances, however, descriptions consist of mixed elements, so that a sunset may be described both spatially as well as by categories. The eyes of the viewpoint character may be said to shift from one part of the sky to another while various features of a sunset, for example, clouds and colors, may be mentioned in terms of categories.

A third type of progression involves a set of discourse elements which are related by virtue of certain logical connections between the parts. There may be temporal factors involved, but the focus in this type of progression is upon the logical relations, not upon temporal sequence. For example, in the statements <u>If he comes I will leave</u> and <u>I will leave if he comes</u> there is a temporal factor, but it is the logical relationship which is in focus, not the temporal sequence.

The logical relations may be roughly classified as dependent, qualificational, and dyadic. Dependent relationships are typically cause-effect, reason-result, means-result, means-purpose, condition-result, ground-implication, and concession-result. Qualificational relationships include generic-specific as well as expressions of manner and setting as they relate to dominant events. Dyadic relationships are primarily additive (<u>and</u>), alternative (<u>or</u>), contrastive (<u>but</u>, <u>except</u>), and comparative (<u>than</u>, <u>as</u>). Discourses in which focal relations are logical constitute what is generally called expository or explanatory discourse.

The fourth basic type of progression consists of dialogue in the sense that the form of response is conditioned by a prior element in the discourse. Two principal types of dialogue are (a) questions and answers and (b) affirmations and negations. The form of a question clearly dictates the form of the response, though not necessarily the content. Similarly, negations of prior affirmations are likewise formally dependent on what has occurred in a previous statement. These two basic types of dialogue are the primary elements of what has been traditionally called "diatribe", a type of progression in which a writer anticipates the kinds of objections which his audience is likely to raise and thus provides answers in advance, though in some instances the actual form of the anticipated objection is also included.

The progression which occurs in dialogue may be strictly limited to a single exchange or it may be multiple as in the case of the literary dialogues of Plato. At the present time the dialogue structure of question and answer is a popular feature of interviews in which reporters provide (often in edited form) the questions and the responses of persons being interviewed. At times, however, the nature of a following question may in fact imply a negation of what an interviewed person has just said, but the overt style of such interviews is still a matter of dialogue based on the question-answer relation.

Rather than consisting of only one major discourse type, most actual texts are mixed. It is rare, for example, that a narrative does not include some description, and often an expository text incorporates a brief narrative (usually for illustrative purposes), while a descriptive analysis of some feature is often a significant element in an expository discourse. Dialogues are often expanded by introducing brief narratives, and they frequently incorporate various sets of logical relations.

The fact that most texts consist of various combinations of basic types of progression is due primarily to the nature of human experience. One seldom speaks of objects without being concerned with both their features (description) and their roles (narrative). Similarly, in the case of events one usually finds it essential to describe settings of time and space to elaborate the circumstances, and to add elements of manner.

While progression accounts for the diversity of elements within a discourse, the factor of cohesion provides the unity. On the macrolevel of rhetorical structure cohesion is attained primarily by thematic unity. That is to say, a single discourse treats a particular topic, though it may, of course, treat such a topic in a diffuse and varied manner. Cohesion also occurs in the unfolding nature of a sequence. Propositions are normally organized in terms of topic and comment in which the topic is essentially old or given information (data shared by both source and receptor) and new information is comment. This type of basic sequence almost inevitably induces a following proposition to pick up the new information and to provide further elaboration or qualification. This type of unfolding structure may relate directly to temporally organized as well as to logically organized sequences. The fact that one element leads into another is an essential part of cohesion. In a sense, one may look upon progression and cohesion, especially on the macrolevel, as being two aspects of the same phenomenon. Progression focuses upon the diversities which occur in a sequence, while cohesion focuses upon the way in which they are tied together.

Cohesion in a discourse is reinforced by features on the microlevel of rhetoric. Situational markers such as here, there, now, then provide spatial and temporal orientations. Referential markers, including personal pronouns, relative pronouns, and deictics, may point forward (cataphoric) or backward (anaphoric) to provide a receptor with constant orientation as to the relationship between the various elements in a discourse.

Repetition as an instrument of cohesion, is of two types: (1) same or similar themes or arrangements of themes and (2) identical or similar sounds, syntactic structures, or lexical units (typically microlevel devices and often having functions quite different from cohesion). The use of the same expression at various points in a discourse, the use of different expressions belonging to the same semantic domain, and even the repetition of propositions having essentially similar meaning (especially at the beginning and the end of a section) may all contribute to cohesion.

Transitional devices are also valuable features in marking cohesion. By introducing sentences with such expressions as moreover, furthermore, in the same way, and because of this a receptor can more readily note the cohesive relations in the progression of discourse. Hypotactic markers such as when, because, if are also important cohesive features.

As already suggested in the listing of certain microlevel features which reinforce the cohesion in texts, it is essential that careful consideration be given to the manner in which these features highlight elements, increase impact, provide esthetic appeal, enlarge semantic ranges, and indicate shifts in intention. It is important, however, that these devices be treated not primarily in terms of these formal features, but on the basis of the processes, which provides the semiotic significance, as treated in considerable detail in chapter two.

Though the Greeks themselves did not distinguish clearly between a microlevel and a macrolevel of rhetoric, nevertheless they certainly did discuss various features characteristic of these levels.[8] One important distinction, normally on a microlevel, was the difference between λέξις εἰρομένη and κατεστραμμένη. The term εἰρομένη referred to a stylistic structure in which clauses and sentences were simply strung together, either without conjunctions (in a so-called "paratactic arrangement") or combined with coordinate conjunctions. The κατεστραμμένη style was essentially a hypotactic style with a great deal of subordination and frequently extensive embedding. In connection with the κατεστραμμένη style, much attention was paid to so-called periodic structures in which a concept was neatly organized so that the beginning and the end exhibited a conceptual or formal unity. The term κατεστραμμένη (literally, 'having turned back') arose from the context of a racetrack in which the contestants rounded the marker and returned to where they had begun.

---

8   For a detailed treatment of the ancient view of variation and variety in rhetorical features, see H. L. F. Drijepondt, 1979, Die antike Theorie der Varietas.

Ancient rhetoricians, however, were not oblivious of the macrolevel of rhetorical structure. The Greek rhetoricians spoke of εὕρεσις and οἰκονομία, two basic concepts which the Roman rhetoricians called inventio and expositio respectively. Inventio referred to the creation of a concept, and the expositio was the manner in which the major outlines of the discourse were formulated.

Though early Greek rhetoricians often spoke in terms of a high or low style, Theophrastus, who succeeded Aristotle, developed the distinction into a system of three levels: plain, intermediate (later called "elegant" by Demetrius), and elevated. Demetrius in the first century A.D. added a fourth type of style, namely "forceful". Both Demetrius and Dionysius of Halicarnassus wrote at length concerning various rhetorical structures and devices, and their insights are important. Unfortunately, however, their analyses are frequently contradictory or faulty, largely because they lacked insight into the structures of non-Indo-European languages. If they had only had a wider base for comparison than what was afforded by Greek and Latin, they no doubt would have been able to develop far more precise definitions and descriptions. They were, however, far more interested in certain qualities of style than in detailed analysis. These qualities of style (called ἀρεταὶ τῆς λέξεως) were thought to consist primarily of ἑλληνισμός (purity of grammar and diction), σαφήνεια (clarity of expression), πρέπον (appropriateness, both in terms of subject matter and setting), κόσμος (the esthetic quality of diction), and finally συντομία (brevity of expression).

One of the problems faced by ancient rhetoricians in dealing with rhetorical structures and stylistic levels was their attempt to define differences primarily in terms of necessary and sufficient features which would clearly delineate distinct categories. In this they largely failed because some of the same rhetorical devices were used in several or

even all of the plain, forceful, elegant, and elevated types
of discourse. If they had only based their definitions on
the variety and the density of features, they could have far
more satisfactorily discussed the significant differences.

It would be wrong, however, to suggest that all classical
rhetoricians were in agreement with regard to the number and
relative value of various rhetorical styles. In the early
period of Greek rhetoric, and particularly in the fifth
century B.C., the elaborate style of Gorgias was greatly
appreciated. Gradually, however, more and more attention
was paid to the plain or forceful styles, so that by the
time of Dionysius of Halicarnassus (first century A.D.), the
plain, straightforward style seemed to be more popular. But
within a century or so, highly elaborate rhetorical devices
were again in vogue, as some of the panegyrics of late
Hellenistic times so clearly demonstrate.

As the subtitle of this volume indicates, the purpose of
this book is to deal with the dimensions of discourse primarily in relationship to rhetorical features in the New
Testament. It is, however, an introduction to a number of
issues and is not by any means an exhaustive treatment. It
does attempt to indicate the influence of rhetorical principles and practice of Hellenistic times, but it is also
oriented to a somewhat broader framework of present-day
literary analysis, in which rhetorical features are stated
primarily in terms of their function, as signs in a semiotic
sense. However, the semiotic framework in which rhetorical
features can perhaps be best analyzed should really be
called a "socio-semiotic framework", for the signs only have
significance in terms of the cultural or social context in
which communication takes place. Within this socio-semiotic
framework, special attention is paid to the functions of
rhetorical structures. In moving from one language to
another it is quite impossible to match rhetorical devices,
but one can deal meaningfully with rhetorical functions,

since these are universals.

Chapter 2 deals with the variety of rhetorical features, not in terms of a list of the more or less forty principal devices discussed by Hellenistic rhetoricians and found in large measure in the New Testament. Rather, the approach involves a discussion of the fundamental formal arrangements, the operation of these at various levels, and an analysis of their functional significance. Chapter 3 deals with the way in which various rhetorical features are characteristic of different types of texts, that is to say, diverse genres. But the treatment of diverse genres focuses on the communicative function of the genres, that is to say, their socio-semiotic significance. Chapters 4 through 7 treat primarily different aspects of meaning, with Chapter 4 concentrating on the meaning of lexical and discourse units. Chapter 5 extends the concept of meaning to those referents of verbal signs which in themselves also constitute signs of secondary or even tertiary levels of meaning. For example, the verbal sign cross has as a referent a particular artifact on which ancient criminals were executed, but the form of that artifact is itself a sign of a Christian institution. In discussing the meaning of words, it is imperative that a clear distinction be made between the referent of a lexical unit and the function of such a referent (whether object, event, or abstract) as a sign relating to a further referent.

Chapter 6 deals with the meaning of nuclear structures, in other words, the meaningful relationships to be found in a nucleus consisting of an event or state and the participants which form a set of satellites related to such a nucleus. This chapter constitutes a type of preparation for the more important analysis of the meaning of internuclear structures in Chapter 7. The meaning of such internuclear structures is analyzed on various levels -- from the level of interclausal structures to the relationship between chapters of a book. These various levels are also viewed from the standpoint of syntactic, semantic, and rhetorical perspectives and are illustrated by a number of New Testament texts.

Chapter 8 is concerned with methods for analyzing the formal and semantic features of texts, and Chapter 9 treats the functions of communication and the interpretative process. Chapter 10 deals with various theories of literary analysis, the relation of language to literature, and the distinctive problems associated with both primary and secondary religious language, while Chapter 11 discusses briefly the implication of rhetoric for translating New Testament texts.

CHAPTER 2

Rhetorical Structures

For many persons the phrase "rhetorical structures" suggests such features of text as unusual organization of sentences, details of antithetical expressions, and possibly sound symbolism. In any event, rhetoric seems to be related primarily to the microlevel structures of a text. When a rhetorical structure such as parallelism is mentioned, persons think usually of juxtaposed clauses having essentially the same meaning and of parallel syntactic structures. Rarely, however, does the term parallelism suggest a parallel organization of two related chapters in a book. This preoccupation with rhetorical features on a microlevel of structure has in many respects clouded important issues and failed to provide a fully satisfactory understanding of the nature of rhetorical structures.

The Greek and Roman rhetoricians, as well as their modern equivalents (usually called literary critics), paid primary attention to the microlevel structures, and in doing so they elaborated a lengthy series of classificatory terms to characterize a number of rhetorical features. Ancient rhetoricians defined, described, and argued about such matters as anthypallage, asyndeton, anadiplosis, paraleipsis, aposiopesis, and antistrophe. The numerous terms and descriptive phrases finally can be analyzed in terms of approximately a hundred different rhetorical devices, of which about forty are especially significant for the New Testament. In this chapter, however, no attempt is made to treat all of the diverse rhetorical devices, nor is there any attempt to define what the Greek rhetoricians meant by various terms.[9]

---

9   For a detailed analysis of these various features, see the outline prepared by Andries Snyman and Kobus Cronje and incorporated in the appendix to this volume.

In the first place, there were considerable differences of opinion as to what terms should be applied to a particular feature, and often the definitions that were employed by Greek rhetoricians fluctuated, depending upon whether formal or functional aspects were being considered.

Rather than deal exhaustively with all of the rhetorical features in the New Testament, it seems far more relevant to select the more important ones and to describe these, first in terms of the formal structures and then in terms of certain significant functions based upon several fundamental relations, including, for example, the relation of parts of a text to one another and the relation of a text to its setting, including, of course, the participants in a particular discourse. This emphasis upon the function of rhetorical structures is in many respects far more important than an analysis of formal features, for what is important is to know how the diverse rhetorical devices contribute to the effectiveness and acceptability of a text in terms of impact and appeal.

The numerous rhetorical features can be readily classified on the basis of four fundamental types: repetition, omission, shifts in expectancy, and compactness. Repetitions may be regarded as additions, and omissions as subtractions, while shifts in expectancies can be described in terms of significant increases in so-called "markedness", that is, the manner in which particular meanings are contextually highlighted. Compactness is a particularly important aspect of ancient rhetoric, in which great emphasis was placed upon conciseness of utterance. The more a speaker or writer can pack into a few words the greater is the impact and appeal, as well as the likelihood that the content will be remembered.

Repetitions
Repetitions are clearly the most obvious rhetorical devices,

and they are the most often commented on, though they are
not necessarily the most frequently occurring features of a
text. Such repetitions, however, may involve almost any
unit of discourse from sounds to series of propositions. In
the Old Testament repetitions of even complete sections are
quite frequent. This is particularly true in the case of
the construction of the tabernacle (Exodus 26 and 36), in
which the series of instructions as to how the tabernacle
was to be constructed and how later it was actually made
involve extensive repetition, but the duplication does serve
to emphasize the importance of details.

Repetitions can probably be best classified in terms of
sounds, grammatical constructions, lexical units, and propositions.

Repetition of sounds involves two principal differences:
(1) those in which there is no special meaningful relationship attached to the lexical units and (2) those in which
similarities of sound correspond to a play on the meanings
of words. In Hebrews 1.1 the participial phrase πολυμερῶς
καὶ πολυτρόπως πάλαι ὁ θεὸς λαλήσας τοῖς πατράσιν ἐν τοῖς
προφήταις contains five words beginning with the sound of π,
five occurrences of λ, and two adverbial endings in -ως.
These serve to illustrate what is no doubt an intentional
repetition of sound. In the New Testament, however, there
is relatively little of this type of phonemic or graphemic
repetition. Far more of this type of repetition occurs in
the Old Testament Hebrew text and especially in poetic discourses.

In a number of instances similarity of sound may also involve similar or contrastive meanings. Note, for example,
the following sequences: φθόνου φόνου 'jealousy, murder'
(Romans 1.29); ἀσυνέτους, ἀσυνθέτους 'without a conscience,
failing to keep promises' (Romans 1.31); and λιμοὶ καὶ
λοιμοί 'famines, plagues,' (Luke 21.11).

The repetition of grammatical constructions involving either lexically distinct or similar elements is quite common in the New Testament. In Matthew 7.7 there is a typical instance of a triple repetition of a grammatical construction involving an imperative followed by a future tense. In two instances the future tense is passive, and in the other instance the future tense may be regarded as semantically passive, since the subject is the beneficiary of the event: αἰτεῖτε, καὶ δοθήσεται ὑμῖν· ζητεῖτε, καὶ εὑρήσετε· κρούετε, καὶ ἀνοιγήσεται ὑμῖν 'ask and it will be given to you; seek and you will find; knock and it will be opened to you'.

In 1 John 2.12-14 the first two words in each principal line are identical with the exception of tense, and the third word in each case belongs to the same semantic domain. There are some additional lexical identities as well as semantic parallels, but what is striking about this series of six expressions is the almost monotonous repetition of the grammatical structures:

γράφω ὑμῖν, τεκνία,
    ὅτι ἀφέωνται ὑμῖν αἱ ἁμαρτίαι διὰ τὸ ὄνομα αὐτοῦ.
γράφω ὑμῖν, πατέρες,
    ὅτι ἐγνώκατε τὸν ἀπ᾽ ἀρχῆς.
γράφω ὑμῖν, νεανίσκοι,
    ὅτι νενικήκατε τὸν πονηρόν.
ἔγραψα ὑμῖν, παιδία,
    ὅτι ἐγνώκατε τὸν πατέρα.
ἔγραψα ὑμῖν, πατέρες,
    ὅτι ἐγνώκατε τὸν ἀπ᾽ ἀρχῆς.
ἔγραψα ὑμῖν, νεανίσκοι,
    ὅτι ἰσχυροί ἐστε
      καὶ ὁ λόγος τοῦ θεοῦ ἐν ὑμῖν μένει
        καὶ νενικήκατε τὸν πονηρόν.

    'I write to you, children,
      because your sins have been forgiven on account of
      his name.

I write to you, fathers,
     because you have known him who is from the be-
          ginning.
I write to you, young men,
     because you have been victorious over the evil
          one.
I wrote to you, children,
     because you have known the father.
I wrote to you, fathers,
     because you have known the one who existed from
          the beginning.
I wrote to you, young men,
     because you are strong
          and the word of God remains in you
               and you have been victorious over the evil one.'

The repetition of lexical units, whether words, phrases, or complete propositions, consists of a number of subtypes. Most commonly the words are identical in both form and meaning, but in a number of instances different words are used but with closely related meanings. Most frequently the lexical units consist of single words, which may occur (a) contiguous with one another or (b) noncontiguous but in corresponding structural positions. In some instances the same word is repeated but with a strikingly different meaning. There are an almost unlimited number of possibilities for such patterns of repetition, but the following are those which occur most frequently in the New Testament.

Repetition of single words contiguous to one another and in the same grammatical construction are clearly emphatic, as in the case of κύριε κύριε 'lord, lord' (Luke 6.46) and σταύρου, σταύρου αὐτόν 'crucify, crucify him' (Luke 23.21).

Words may also be repeated in a noncontiguous relation but in corresponding structural positions. In 1 Corinthians 13.7, for example, the term πάντα ('all things') is repeated in an initial position with four verbs: πάντα στέγει, πάντα πιστεύει, πάντα ἐλπίζει, πάντα ὑπομένει 'bears all things, believes all things, hopes all things, endures all things'. The final position in corresponding clauses may not be quite as emphatic, but it is significant, as, for example, in Hebrews 2.16: οὐ γὰρ δήπου ἀγγέλων ἐπιλαμβάνεται, ἀλλὰ σπέρματος Ἀβραὰμ ἐπιλαμβάνεται 'for clearly he does not help the angels, but he helps the descendants of Abraham'. Note another instance of repetition in final position in 1 Corinthians 10.31: εἴτε οὖν ἐσθίετε εἴτε πίνετε εἴτε τι ποιεῖτε, πάντα εἰς δόξαν θεοῦ ποιεῖτε 'therefore, whether you eat or drink or whatever you do, do all to the glory of God'.

In some instances repetition occurs in both initial and final position as in 1 Corinthians 10.21: οὐ δύνασθε ποτήριον κυρίου πίνειν καὶ ποτήριον δαιμονίων· οὐ δύνασθε τραπέζης κυρίου μετέχειν καὶ τραπέζης δαιμονίων 'you are not able to drink the cup of the Lord and the cup of demons; you are not able to share in the table of the Lord and in the table of demons'.

One favored device among classical rhetoricians was to end an expression with a word and to begin the following expression with the same word. This has been done with some slight variations in Romans 5.3b-5a: ἡ θλῖψις ὑπομονὴν κατεργάζεται, ἡ δὲ ὑπομονὴ δοκιμήν, ἡ δὲ δοκιμὴ ἐλπίδα, ἡ δὲ ἐλπὶς οὐ καταισχύνει 'trouble produces endurance, endurance produces approval, and approval produces hope, and hope does not disappoint'. In John 1.1 a similar rhetorical arrangement occurs: ἐν ἀρχῇ ἦν ὁ λόγος, καὶ ὁ λόγος ἦν πρὸς τὸν θεόν, καὶ θεὸς ἦν ὁ λόγος 'in the beginning was the word, the word was with God, and the word was God'. In John 1.1 one should note that for the sake of the rhetorical patterning the predicate element θεός is put in initial position in the third clause, but it exists without an article and thus is clearly marked as predicate in meaning. In Romans 8.30 the repetitive series of verbs represents an a b b c c d set, while the pronominal markers οὕς ... τούτους occur three times: οὓς δὲ προώρισεν, τούτους καὶ ἐκάλεσεν, καὶ οὓς ἐκάλεσεν, τούτους καὶ ἐδικαίωσεν, οὓς δὲ ἐδικαίωσεν, τούτους καὶ ἐδόξασεν 'whom he set apart he called, and those he called he put right, and those whom he put right he glorified'.

A word may be repeated frequently within a particular section of a discourse but without occurring in certain syntactically corresponding positions. For example, the Greek term σῶμα 'body' occurs seventeen times in 1 Corinthians 12.12-26, an average of more than once in each verse. In 1 Corinthians 15.12-29 the verb ἐγείρομαι occurs nine times. Such a repetition not only marks a theme but adds emphasis.

The repetition of so-called "function words" (words which primarily relate other words or phrases to one another, principally conjunctions or conjunctive adverbs) may be quite distinctive of certain styles. The repeated use of εὐθύς in Mark, whether in a temporal or transitional sense, has often been cited as being typical of Markan style. Perhaps even more indicative of distinctive Markan usage is the repetition of καί as introductory to complete sentences. For example, in Mark 3 only three sentences out of twenty-three do not begin with καί. Though it is true that in some of the best Greek writers almost all sentences begin with some kind of conjunction (whether initial or postpositive), this excessive use of καί, almost to the exclusion of such typical Greek conjunctions as δέ, γάρ, and οὖν, suggests a kind of Semiticized Greek under the influence of Hebrew vav.

The repetition of the same word but in a distinctly different meaning occurs frequently in the New Testament and is perhaps best illustrated by John 1.1, in which ἦν occurs three times with three different meanings: 'to exist', 'to be in a place', and 'to have the nature of'. In John 3.8 πνεῦμα first occurs in the meaning of 'wind', but at the end of verse eight πνεῦμα clearly denotes the Holy Spirit.

The repetition of the same phrase, particularly in an
initial position, is rhetorically emphatic as in the case of
ἐὰν εἴπωμεν ὅτι 'if we say that' in 1 John 1.6, 8, 10. In
Matthew 5.22, 28, 32, 34, 39, and 44 the initial phrase ἐγὼ
δὲ λέγω ὑμῖν is emphatic.

In some instances the same words may be repeated but in a
different grammatical construction and with a resulting difference in meaning between the two clauses. In Mark 2.27,
for example, the two clauses are contrastive and the order
is reversed, thus providing a chiastic structure: τὸ
σάββατον διὰ τὸν ἄνθρωπον ἐγένετο καὶ οὐχ ὁ ἄνθρωπος διὰ τὸ
σάββατον 'the Sabbath was made for man and not man for the
Sabbath'.

In many instances repetition involves not the same words but
different words having closely related meanings. Typical
phrases of this type introduce direct discourse. Such expressions may be contiguous or simply relatively close to
one another. Compare, for example, ἠτήσατο λέγουσα 'asked
saying' (Mark 6.25), ἀποκριθεὶς αὐτοῖς λέγει 'answering
them, he said' (Mark 9.19), and κράξας ὁ πατὴρ τοῦ παιδίου
ἔλεγεν 'the father of the boy crying out said' (Mark 9.24).

In some instances there is a repetition of certain semantic
components so that the resulting expression may be regarded
as involving redundancy or more probably emphasis. Compare,
for example, Galatians 1.17 πάλιν ὑπέστρεψα 'I returned
again' and Acts 18.21 πάλιν ἀνακάμψω 'I will return
again' , in which πάλιν duplicates the meaning of the respective prefixes.

The use of different words with closely related meanings
appears to be a device for enlarging somewhat the scope of
reference of a statement. In 1 John 1.1, for example,
ἑωράκαμεν and ἐθεασάμεθα are closely related, though of
course not identical in meaning. They do, however, mutually

reinforce the notion of visual experience. In Matthew 5.45 the phrases ἐπὶ πονηροὺς καὶ ἀγαθοὺς and ἐπὶ δικαίους καὶ ἀδίκους clearly refer to the same types of persons on whom God makes the sun rise and the rain fall, though in the order of words there is a chiastic arrangement in the semantic parallels. One may, of course, translate as 'the evil and the good' and 'the righteous and the unrighteous', but the reference is obviously the same.

The use of close synonyms may, however, be designed primarily for the sake of variety rather than for any distinctiveness in meaning. Such repetitions of words closely related in meaning is typical of the Johannine writings. Alternations between λέγω and λαλέω ('to speak'), οἶδα and γινώσκω ('to know'), and ὁράω and βλέπω ('to see') are illustrative. It is difficult to know whether in the case of φιλέω and ἀγαπάω ('to love') in John 21.15-19 one is to treat the differences as semantically or rhetorically significant, though most scholars opt for the latter.

The use of different words with antithetical meanings (that is to say, words in which the meanings are in polar contrast, that is, often representing positive or negative features within the same semantic domain) is a common feature of ancient rhetoric. In the New Testament considerable use is made of such contrasts. In John 1.5 the distinction is between φῶς 'light' and σκοτία 'darkness'. Note the same contrast between φῶς and σκοτία in 1 John 1.5. Compare also ψεύστης 'liar' and ἡ ἀλήθεια 'truth' in 1 John 2.4. Note also ὁ ἀρνούμενος 'one who denies' and ὁ ὁμολογῶν 'one who confesses' in 1 John 2.23.

In Romans 8.38-39 there are a number of polar contrasts, for example, θάνατος 'death' and ζωή 'life', ἐνεστῶτα 'things present' and μέλλοντα 'things in the future', ὕψωμα 'height' and βάθος 'depth'.

The use of what are called semantic reciprocals may also prove an effective rhetorical device, especially when such reciprocals are placed close to one another, for example, ὅσοι δὲ ἔλαβον αὐτόν, ἔδωκεν αὐτοῖς 'for as many as received him, he gave to them' (John 1.12). Reciprocal relations may also be expressed in terms of active and passive meanings. Compare, for example, οἱ ἐλεήμονες 'those who show mercy' and ἐλεηθήσονται 'they will receive mercy' (Matthew 5.7).

In some instances significant rhetorical impact is gained by the use of different words based on the same root. For example, in 1 John 2.18-27 there is a significant interplay between ἀντίχριστος 'antiChrist', Χριστός 'Christ', and χρῖσμα 'anointing'.

Even the repetition of the same morphological structures may be rhetorically significant, as in 1 Corinthians 15.44-49, which makes effective use of the adjectival derivatives ψυχικός 'natural', πνευματικός 'spiritual', χοϊκός 'earthly', and ἐπουράνιος 'heavenly'.

Repetition may involve complete propositions, but rarely are such repetitions identical. One almost identical occurrence has already been noted, 1 John 2.13 and 14: ἔγραψα (γράφω, verse 13) ὑμῖν, πατέρες, ὅτι ἐγνώκατε τὸν ἀπ᾽ ἀρχῆς 'I wrote to you, fathers, because you have known the one who existed from the beginning'.

Usually the repetition of the same idea is expressed in slightly different ways. Compare, for example, 1 Corinthians 12.12 and 20: τὸ σῶμα ἕν ἐστιν καὶ μέλη πολλὰ ἔχει 'the body is one and has many parts' and πολλὰ μὲν μέλη, ἓν δὲ σῶμα 'many parts but one body'. Essentially the same ideas may be expressed but with different illustrative examples. Compare, for example, the two statements in 1 Corinthians 12.17: εἰ ὅλον τὸ σῶμα ὀφθαλμός, ποῦ ἡ ἀκοή; εἰ ὅλον ἀκοή, ποῦ ἡ ὄσφρησις; 'if the whole body were the eye,

where would the hearing be? If the whole body were hearing,
where would be the sense of smelling?'

One type of repetition involves a significant reversal of
roles. In 1 John 4.10, for example, οὐχ ὅτι ἡμεῖς
ἠγαπήκαμεν τὸν θεόν, ἀλλ' ὅτι αὐτὸς ἠγάπησεν ἡμᾶς 'not that
we love God but that he loves us', there is a repetition of
components but in a completely reversed relationship. Compare 1 John 4.15b, ὁ θεὸς ἐν αὐτῷ μένει καὶ αὐτὸς ἐν τῷ θεῷ
'God remains in him and he in God'. Compare also 1 John
4.16b, ἐν τῷ θεῷ μένει καὶ ὁ θεὸς ἐν αὐτῷ μένει 'he remains
in God and God remains in him', and 1 John 4.19, ἡμεῖς
ἀγαπῶμεν, ὅτι αὐτὸς πρῶτος ἠγάπησεν ἡμᾶς 'we love because he
first loved us'.

Another type of propositional repetition involves positive/
negative contrast, something which is conspicuous in the
Johannine writings, for example, πάντα δι' αὐτοῦ ἐγένετο,
καὶ χωρὶς αὐτοῦ ἐγένετο οὐδὲ ἕν 'all things came into existence through him, and without him not anything came into
existence' (John 1.3), or καὶ ὡμολόγησεν καὶ οὐκ ἠρνήσατο
'and he confessed and he did not deny' (John 1.20), or οὐ
ζητῶ τὸ θέλημα τὸ ἐμὸν ἀλλὰ τὸ θέλημα τοῦ πέμψαντός με 'I do
not seek my own will but the will of the one who sent me'
(John 5.30). Such contrastive statements also occur in the
Pauline Epistles, for example, ἀλήθειαν λέγω ἐν Χριστῷ, οὐ
ψεύδομαι 'I tell the truth in Christ, I do not lie' (Romans
9.1).

A special type of repetition is involved in allusions and
quotations. This is an aspect of what may be called intertextuality, that is to say, the relationship between texts.
The allusion may be relatively subtle, as in the case of
John 1.1, in which the phrase ἐν ἀρχῇ 'in the beginning' is
a rhetorical echo of the beginning of Genesis, especially
since this relationship is reinforced by statements concerning the role of the λόγος 'the Word' in creation in John

1.3.

One may also encounter series of allusions as in Mary's song of praise in Luke 1.47-55, and in the prophecy of Zechariah in Luke 1.68-79. These two hymnic discourses constitute a pastiche of phrases drawn from various parts of the Old Testament or are based upon similar expressions occurring in various Old Testament texts.

Actual quotations in the New Testament are frequent, and though these are for the most part based upon the Septuagint Greek text, some reflect the Hebrew text and often the quotations are not exact but are semantically and syntactically adjusted to the New Testament writings. Compare, for example, the treatment of the quotation from Psalm 118.25-26 in Matthew 21.9, Ὡσαννὰ τῷ υἱῷ Δαυίδ· Εὐλογημένος ὁ ἐρχόμενος ἐν ὀνόματι κυρίου· Ὡσαννὰ ἐν τοῖς ὑψίστοις, with the reduced form of that quotation in Matthew 23.39, Εὐλογημένος ὁ ἐρχόμενος ἐν ὀνόματι κυρίου. In Romans 1.17 the omission of μου 'my' certainly facilitates the interpretation which Paul gives to this expression. In Hebrews 10.38 this same passage is rendered as ὁ δὲ δίκαιός μου ἐκ πίστεως ζήσεται, with the occurrence of μου, but in a different grammatical relationship. A significant difference in the meaning of a quotation may depend upon whether it is a quotation from the Greek Septuagint translation or from the Hebrew text itself. In Hebrews 1.7, ὁ ποιῶν τοὺς ἀγγέλους αὐτοῦ πνεύματα, καὶ τοὺς λειτουργοὺς αὐτοῦ πυρὸς φλόγα 'he makes his angels winds and his servants flames of fire' comes from the Septuagint text rather than from the Hebrew, which means 'you make the winds your messengers and make fire and flame your ministers'.

Omissions

Omissions, the second major class of rhetorical features, may be regarded as having "zero significance", that is to say, a significant absence of something. These omissions are essentially of two major types: (1) those which involve omissions which can readily be supplied from the context and (2) those which cannot be readily supplied from the context. The most common kind of omissions are syntactic ellipses, and these more often than not involve the omission of so-called function words, that is to say, words which serve to relate textual elements to one another. In Romans 2.28-29 the verb ἐστιν is omitted at least three times. The omissions are not syntactically required but are optional. The omissions do serve to make the text somewhat more concise and at the same time serve to heighten the contrasts: οὐ γὰρ ὁ ἐν τῷ φανερῷ Ἰουδαῖός ἐστιν, οὐδὲ ἡ ἐν τῷ φανερῷ ἐν σαρκὶ περιτομή· ἀλλ' ὁ ἐν τῷ κρυπτῷ Ἰουδαῖος, καὶ περιτομὴ καρδίας ἐν πνεύματι οὐ γράμματι, οὗ ὁ ἔπαινος οὐκ ἐξ ἀνθρώπων ἀλλ' ἐκ τοῦ θεοῦ 'for he is not a Jew who is one merely by appearance, nor is circumcision merely a matter of physical appearance; but a Jew is one who is a Jew on the inside, whose heart is circumcised by the spirit and not by the written law; his praise is not from people but from God' (Romans 2.28-29).

An important element in the stylistic effectiveness of 1 Corinthians 13 consists of a number of omissions of conjunctions, particularly the conjunction καί. For example, in 1 Corinthians 13.4-7 there are thirteen omissions of καί: ἡ ἀγάπη μακροθυμεῖ, χρηστεύεται ἡ ἀγάπη, οὐ ζηλοῖ, ἡ ἀγάπη οὐ περπερεύεται, οὐ φυσιοῦται, οὐκ ἀσχημονεῖ, οὐ ζητεῖ τὰ ἑαυτῆς, οὐ παροξύνεται, οὐ λογίζεται τὸ κακόν, οὐ χαίρει ἐπὶ τῇ ἀδικίᾳ, συγχαίρει δὲ τῇ ἀληθείᾳ. πάντα στέγει, πάντα πιστεύει, πάντα ἐλπίζει, πάντα ὑπομένει 'love is patient, kind; it is not jealous, nor conceited, nor proud, nor ill-mannered, nor seeks its own, nor irritable, nor keeps a record of wrong, nor rejoices in evil but rejoices in the truth; bears all things, believes all things, hopes all things, endures all things'. The effectiveness of the ommission of καί in these verses in 1 Corinthians 13 in the Greek text does not mean, however, that a similar omission in a translation would prove to be equally effective. In fact, a literal translation usually sounds awkward. It is rarely possible to match in other languages the same patterns of parallelism and word classes.

The omission of so-called referential vocabulary (in contrast with so-called function words) involves far greater complications in structure, but such omissions are often made for the sake of stylistic variation. In Hebrews 1.5, 8, and 10 there are several rather heavy omissions. Note, for example, that at the beginning of verse 5 the clause τίνι γὰρ εἶπέν ποτε τῶν ἀγγέλων 'for to whom of the angels did he ever say' is reduced simply to καὶ πάλιν 'and again' in the second half of verse 5. In verse 7 the introductory clause is καὶ πρὸς μὲν τοὺς ἀγγέλους λέγει 'and to the angels he says', which becomes at the beginning of verse 8 simply πρὸς δὲ τὸν υἱόν 'but to the son', and at the beginning of verse 10 there is a still further reduction to καί 'and'. In Matthew 25.22 there is a rather strange omission which can, however, readily be supplied from the preceding context, but in isolation the first part of verse 22 seems strange: προσελθὼν δὲ καὶ ὁ τὰ δύο τάλαντα εἶπεν. Only by the introduction of λαβών from verse 20 can one meaningfully translate this clause as 'also the one who had received the two talents came and said'.

In some instances omissions involve a verb which is different from the one in the immediately preceding context, but one which nevertheless belongs essentially to the same semantic domain. In 1 Corinthians 3.2 γάλα ὑμᾶς ἐπότισα, οὐ βρῶμα 'I gave you milk to drink, not meat', clearly one cannot use ἐπότισα with βρῶμα. An appropriate verb form would be ἐψώμισα, which does occur with edible substances such as meat or other solid foods.

In some instances omissions may be the result of calculated avoidance based on cultural attitudes or values. For the

New Testament such avoidance is characteristic of references to deity. In Matthew 7.1 μὴ κρίνετε, ἵνα μὴ κριθῆτε, literally 'do not judge, in order that you may not be judged', a strictly word-for-word rendering may miss the point of judgement being divine judgement rather than merely advice not to criticize people so as to avoid criticism.

There appears to be no instance of an omission in the New Testament which cannot be supplied from the immediate context or from one's knowledge of patterns of cultural avoidance.

In some instances it is possible to employ an omission which has far greater impact than if one had completed a statement. For example, one might say in English If you do this, I'll .... Because of its indeterminacy such a threat carries far more impact than if one had actually specified the consequence of such a conditional statement. Compare the unfinished condition in Mark 9.22-23.

Shifts in Expectancy

Shifts, whether in word order, sentence structure, or of lexical meaning, are some of the more effective rhetorical features. They depend for their significance on the fact that the reader recognizes the unusual word order, syntactic structure, or meaning of a word, phrase, or complete sentence. Accordingly, such shifts involve an increase in markedness. The tension which is introduced in such shifts between the normal and the non-normal, between the usual and the unusual, between the expected and the unexpected, accounts for the significantly greater impact involved in such shifts.

In James 1.2 the occurrence of πᾶσαν χαράν ('all joy') right at the beginning of a sentence which speaks of 'all kinds of difficulties' clearly carries considerable impact, for one would certainly expect quite a different order, for example, ἀδελφοί μου, ὅταν πειρασμοῖς περιπέσητε ποικίλοις ἡγήσασθε πᾶσαν χαράν, rather than the startling order which does occur, namely, πᾶσαν χαρὰν ἡγήσασθε, ἀδελφοί μου, ὅταν πειρασμοῖς περιπέσητε ποικίλοις. To duplicate something of this type of word order in James 1.2 one might translate 'how completely fortunate you should consider yourselves, my brothers, when you encounter all kinds of trials'. In the beatitudes, the initial position of μακάριοι likewise marks an important shift.

In some instances it is the shifting of a word outside of its normal position within a clause which heightens its relevance. In Matthew 6.28b the position of τὰ κρίνα τοῦ ἀγροῦ 'flowers of the field' outside of the clause πῶς αὐξάνουσιν 'how they grow' serves to focus greater attention upon the flowers of the field.

Embedding parenthetical material in a sentence clearly involves a disruption in the syntactic patterning, but such embedding can be rhetorically significant. In Romans 1.13 the clause καὶ ἐκωλύθην ἄχρι τοῦ δεῦρο 'but I have been prevented up to the present' is clearly parenthetical, for the following clause, ἵνα τινὰ καρπὸν σχῶ καὶ ἐν ὑμῖν 'in order that I might have some results among you', does not refer to the immediately preceding clause but to the first part of verse 13.

In 2 Corinthians 11.21b the phrase ἐν ἀφροσύνῃ λέγω 'I am talking like a fool' stands in a parenthetical relationship to the preceding and following expressions, ἐν ᾧ δ' ἄν τις τολμᾷ...τολμῶ κἀγώ 'in so far as anyone may dare to boast... I also dare'. Clearly, the interruption of a sentence structure by the intrusion of an explanatory expression is bound to carry considerable impact.

Shifts in sentence structure are often regarded as grammatical errors, since a sentence begins with one type of

structure but shifts to another structure or is broken off
and another sentence takes over. Such shifts in sentence
structure, often called anacolutha, will, of course, be
either unintentional or intentional, but they are rarely to
be interpreted as grammatical errors. In the case of the
Pauline writings, such shifts in sentence structure may reflect Paul's overwhelming involvement in the subject matter.
Being so full of the subject and so impressed by the urgency
of the message, Paul may have shifted sentence structure
without intentionally doing so. This may very well be the
case in Galatians 2.6: ἀπὸ δὲ τῶν δοκούντων εἶναί τι --
ὁποῖοί ποτε ἦσαν οὐδέν μοι διαφέρει· πρόσωπον ὁ θεὸς
ἀνθρώπου οὐ λαμβάνει -- ἐμοὶ γὰρ οἱ δοκοῦντες οὐδὲν
προσανέθεντο 'but those who seemed to be leaders -- I say
this because it makes no difference to me what they were;
God does not judge by outward appearances -- for those
leaders made no new suggestions to me'. A similar type of
grammatical shift occurs in Romans 5.12-13: διὰ τοῦτο ὥσπερ
δι' ἑνὸς ἀνθρώπου ἡ ἁμαρτία εἰς τὸν κόσμον εἰσῆλθεν καὶ διὰ
τῆς ἁμαρτίας ὁ θάνατος, καὶ οὕτως εἰς πάντας ἀνθρώπους ὁ
θάνατος διῆλθεν, ἐφ' ᾧ πάντες ἥμαρτον -- ἄχρι γὰρ νόμου
ἁμαρτία ἦν ἐν κόσμῳ, ἁμαρτία δὲ οὐκ ἐλλογεῖται μὴ ὄντος
νόμου 'therefore as sin came into the world through one man
and death through sin, and so death spread to all people, on
the basis that all sinned -- for before the law sin was in
the world, but sin was not stipulated as sin since the law
did not exist'.

In Acts 1.4, however, there seems to be a clear instance of
a shift in grammatical structure for the sake of emphasis.
In the first part of verse 4, the reference is to the third
person, but in the clause ἣν ἠκούσατέ μου the shift is to
the second person, and this provides the basis for a shift
to the second person in verse 5: καὶ συναλιζόμενος
παρήγγειλεν αὐτοῖς ἀπὸ Ἱεροσολύμων μὴ χωρίζεσθαι, ἀλλὰ
περιμένειν τὴν ἐπαγγελίαν τοῦ πατρὸς ἣν ἠκούσατέ μου· ὅτι
Ἰωάννης μὲν ἐβάπτισεν ὕδατι, ὑμεῖς δὲ ἐν πνεύματι

βαπτισθήσεσθε ἁγίῳ οὐ μετὰ πολλὰς ταύτας ἡμέρας 'and when they came together, he announced that they should not depart from Jerusalem but wait for the promise of the father about which you have heard from me; John baptized with water, but you shall be baptized by the Holy Spirit in a few days' (Acts 1.4-5). Most translations smooth out this shift by rendering the entire statement by Jesus as direct discourse rather than shifting from indirect to direct discourse, but the shift from third to second person in the Greek text certainly increases the impact of the concluding part of this introduction to the book of Acts.

Purposeful use of terms with more than one meaning in a particular context may be regarded as involving a kind of fluctuating semantic shift. In John 3.3 the ambiguity of ἄνωθεν 'from above' or 'again' sets the stage for the initial misinterpretation of the meaning by Nicodemus and the later explanation by Jesus. A similar ambiguity occurs in John 4.10 in the phrase ὕδωρ ζῶν 'living water', which the Samaritan woman interprets in its literal sense of 'running water' in contrast with water from a cistern or a pool. This misinterpretation leads, of course, to a fuller explanation by Jesus in verse 14.

Shifts between verbal content and intent are particularly important rhetorical devices. In these instances the form does not match the function, and there is an essential shift in the communicative significance of what is said. One of the common shifts between content and intent involves socalled rhetorical questions. These are expressions which have the form of a question but are not designed to elicit information. The intent, therefore, is not to ask for a response but to make an emphatic declaration. In Romans 8.31-35 there are a number of these rhetorical questions. In verse 31 when Paul writes τί οὖν ἐροῦμεν πρὸς ταῦτα; 'therefore what shall we say with regard to these things?' there is obviously no request to supply an answer. In the follow-

ing question, εἰ ὁ θεὸς ὑπὲρ ἡμῶν, τίς καθ᾽ ἡμῶν; 'if God
is for us, who can be against us?' again this is not a question asking for information but an emphatic declaration that
'if God is for us, no one can be against us'. In fact, for
most of these rhetorical questions, the text itself provides
an answer. In 1 John 3.17 the question 'How can the love of
God remain in him?' is simply an emphatic way of saying that
such a person cannot really be loving God.

A shift between content and intent may also involve a decla-
rative statement with imperative intent. In 1 John 2.6, ὁ
λέγων ἐν αὐτῷ μένειν ὀφείλει καθὼς ἐκεῖνος περιεπάτησεν καὶ
αὐτὸς οὕτως περιπατεῖν 'whoever says he remains in union
with him ought to live as that one lived'. Though this de-
clarative statement does involve obligation in its literal
form, the intent is clearly imperative.

Classical rhetoricians particularly favored apparent contradictions or paradoxes which could be resolved by the context
and in this way could highlight the significance of something which might otherwise seem impossible. Such an apparent contradiction occurs in 2 Corinthians 3.10. The statement οὐ γὰρ δεδόξασται τὸ δεδοξασμένον 'for that which has
been made glorious has not been made glorious' is clearly
contradictory, but this is resolved by the rest of verse 10.

In 2 Timothy 2.12b-13 there is a strange shift in the logical relationships, so that the first part of verse 13 seems
to involve an apparent contradiction:
  εἰ ἀρνησόμεθα, κἀκεῖνος ἀρνήσεται ἡμᾶς·
  εἰ ἀπιστοῦμεν, ἐκεῖνος πιστὸς μένει,
      ἀρνήσασθαι γὰρ ἑαυτὸν οὐ δύναται.
  'if we deny him, he will deny us;
  if we are not faithful, he remains faithful,
      for he cannot be false to himself'.
There seems to be no logical relationship between the conditional clause εἰ ἀπιστοῦμεν 'if we are not faithful' and the

conclusion, ἐκεῖνος πιστὸς μένει 'he remains faithful', but this seemingly illogical relationship is resolved by the final line, in which ἀρνήσασθαι has quite a different meaning than it has in verse 12b.

An important shift between content and intent involves expressions of irony, for in such statements one does not mean precisely what is said, but the context indicates the shift in intent, for example, 2 Corinthians 12.13: τί γὰρ ἐστιν ὃ ἡσσώθητε ὑπὲρ τὰς λοιπὰς ἐκκλησίας, εἰ μὴ ὅτι αὐτὸς ἐγὼ οὐ κατενάρκησα ὑμῶν; χαρίσασθέ μοι τὴν ἀδικίαν ταύτην 'for how is it that you were treated worse than the other churches, except for the fact that I myself was no burden to you? Forgive me for this injustice.'

Understatement likewise involves a shift between verbal content and communicative intent. Such expressions (commonly called litotes) are emphatic by virtue of their obvious understatement of the case. In Luke 1.37, ὅτι οὐκ ἀδυνατήσει παρὰ τοῦ θεοῦ πᾶν ῥῆμα 'because with God anything is not impossible' is really a declaration that 'God can do anything'. In Romans 10.16 there is likewise an understatement based on a negation: ἀλλ᾽ οὐ πάντες ὑπήκουσαν τῷ εὐαγγελίῳ 'but not all were obedient to the Good News'.

More common than understatement is overstatement, or hyperbole. The statement in Mark 1.33, καὶ ἦν ὅλη ἡ πόλις ἐπισυνηγμένη πρὸς τὴν θύραν 'and the entire city was gathered at the door', is a typical overstatement. Jesus, however, used numerous hyperboles in his teachings. When he spoke of straining out a gnat and swallowing a camel (Matthew 23.24) or of a beam in one's own eye in contrast with a speck in the eye of another (Luke 6.41-42) or of a camel going through the eye of a needle (Matthew 19.24), he was clearly using hyperbole.

One of the most interesting rhetorical devices widely used

by the ancient orators, but occurring only a few times in the New Testament, is the explicit contradiction of an evident communicative intent. In 2 Corinthians 9.1 Paul indicates that it was superfluous for him to write to the Corinthians concerning providing help for fellow believers, but this does not prevent him from going ahead and saying something specifically about this matter. A somewhat similar device occurs in Philemon 19b: ἵνα μὴ λέγω σοι ὅτι καὶ σεαυτόν μοι προσοφείλεις 'I should not have to tell you that you owe your very self to me'.

Significant shifts in meaning from one major semantic domain to another are characteristic of figurative meanings. The less conventionalized such shifts of meaning are, the greater the awareness of the semantic tension between the literal and the figurative meanings. So-called frozen figurative meanings (those in which there is no longer any active awareness of the shift in meaning) are excluded.

The New Testament abounds in the figurative meanings of single words, both metonymies and metaphors. The occurrence of ἄρτος 'bread' (Matthew 6.11) meaning 'nourishment necessary for existence' is a typical case of metonymy, based as it is upon association and in this instance the relation of part for the whole (often called synecdoche, which is generally treated by semioticians as a type of metonymy). The occurrence of περιτομή 'circumcision' (Galatians 2.9) referring to the Jews, ψυχή 'soul' (Acts 2.43) meaning the entire person, and σάρξ, literally 'flesh', (Romans 9.3) as a designation for 'race' are all typical metonymies.

Metaphors based on the principle of similarity are somewhat less common than metonymies but are still quite frequent, for example, ἀλώπηξ 'fox' (Luke 13.32) in reference to Herod, Σατανᾶς 'Satan' (Mark 8.33) as a designation for Peter, and πατήρ 'father' (John 8.44) referring to the devil as the spiritual progenitor of the Jewish leaders.

These metonymies and metaphors are all typical and active
(though conventional) figurative expressions. Some figurative expressions, however, are nonconventional, and they may
be classified as essentially instances of figurative usage
rather than of figurative meanings, that is to say, they
represent quite novel instances of figurative expression. In
Romans 11.17-19 Paul makes extensive use of κλάδος 'branch'
and ῥίζα 'root', referring to the experience and function of
the Jews in relationship to the promises of God. This apparent nonconventional use of figurative expressions is typical of primary religious language,[10] since fresh insights
can seldom be expressed adequately by means of traditional
semantic formulations. The equation of Hagar with the covenant made at Mount Sinai and the identification of that with
the city of Jerusalem in contrast with the heavenly Jerusalem (Galatians 4.24-25) is probably another instance of nonconventional figurative usage.

The New Testament abounds in idioms (expressions consisting
of two or more words, whose meaning is not to be derived
from the sum total of the parts). Expressions such as
ἀναζωσάμενοι τὰς ὀσφύας τῆς διανοίας ὑμῶν 'girding up the
loins of your mind' (1 Peter 1.13), μὴ σαλπίσῃς ἔμπροσθέν
σου 'do not sound a trumpet ahead of you' (Matthew 6.2), and
κηρυχθήσεται ἐπὶ τῶν δωμάτων 'it shall be preached on the
housetops' (Luke 12.3) are all typical idioms for which the
meaning can be readily determined from the general context.
Furthermore, one can rather easily determine the behavioral
basis for such idioms. However, in the case of ἄνθρακας
πυρὸς σωρεύσεις ἐπὶ τὴν κεφαλὴν αὐτοῦ 'you will heap coals
of fire upon his head' (Romans 12.20), it is not possible to
determine precisely the behavioral basis for such an idiom
nor what its meaning really is. Both contexts in which it

---

10   For a discussion of "primary religious language" see
     the first part of Chapter 10.

is employed would seem to suggest this as a means of making someone ashamed of what he has done.

It would, however, be quite wrong to think of figurative meanings as being restricted merely to individual words or idioms. Radical shifts between major semantic classes may also occur with a number of discourse units. Parables, allegories, proverbs, and apocalyptic literature are all figurative expressions, that is to say, there is a difference in meaning between the literal statement and the evident intention of the writer or speaker. The story of the Good Samaritan (Luke 10.25-37) constitutes a message about the second of the two great commandments and is a dramatic indictment of ethnocentric attitudes. Apocalyptic literature is particularly symbolic and figurative, though many persons fail to recognize the figurative meanings and insist upon literal or quasi-literal interpretations.

Compactness

Compactness involves packing into the fewest possible words the maximum amount of meaning. Perhaps the most well-known passage illustrating compactness is 1 Corinthians 13, especially verses 4-8, but as in the case of 1 Corinthians 13, compactness is often combined with other rhetorical features, especially parallelism and ellipsis. Note, for example, the lexical condensation in the first part of the Lord's prayer, in which syntactic and phonetic parallelisms also play important roles (Mt 6.9-10):

ἁγιασθήτω τὸ ὄνομά σου,	your name be kept holy
ἐλθέτω ἡ βασιλεία σου,	your kingdom come
γενηθήτω τὸ θέλημά σου,	your will be done

Compactness is also typical of discourse formulas, as is well illustrated by introductions to letters. The first seven verses of Romans are especially condensed. In fact, it seems almost incredible that so many relevant themes

could be included within a single sentence: Paul's calling,
the relation of the Gospel to the Holy Scriptures, the human
and divine nature of the Son, Christ's resurrection from the
dead, Paul's apostleship to the nations, the fact that the
believers in Rome are loved by God and called to be his
people, and the greetings to the believers based on their
relationship to God and the Lord Jesus Christ.

Creedal formulations also tend to be succinct and compact.
Note, for example, 1 Timothy 3.16b:

'Ὃς ἐφανερώθη ἐν σάρκι,
  ἐδικαιώθη ἐν πνεύματι,
    ὤφθη ἀγγέλοις,
  ἐκηρύχθη ἐν ἔθνεσιν,
    ἐπιστεύθη ἐν κόσμῳ,
      ἀνελήμφθη ἐν δόξῃ.

Who appeared in human form,
    was shown to be right by the Spirit,
        was seen by angels,
    was preached among the nations,
        was believed in throughout the world,
            was taken up into heaven.

This creedal formulation also gains much by its evident
phonetic, verbal, and syntactic parallelism, as well as by
the fact that the progression of events coincides with the
historical order.

Functions of Rhetorical Features

In many respects the functions of rhetorical features are
far more important than their diverse linguistic forms. The
functions and the corresponding significance of such features can best be understood in terms of a number of relations which these rhetorical features serve to mark. The
five most important relations in which rhetorical features
figure importantly are (1) the relationship of parts of a
text to one another, (2) the relationship of a text to the

participants in the communication, (3) the relationship of the text to the setting, in terms of time, place, and audience, (4) the relationship of the text to the real world, and (5) the relationship of the text to other similar texts.

The relationship of parts of a text to one another is essentially an aspect of cohesion, that is to say, the way in which the parts of a text fit together. The repetition of individual lexical units or syntactic structures constitute two important ways in which cohesion is attained. Parallelism also serves to highlight cohesion, and various techniques for foregrounding and backgrounding likewise provide the necessary ingredients for the cohesive structure of a discourse unit. Even plays on the meanings of individual words may serve a cohesive function, and certainly the repetition of propositions, whether in exactly the same form or in slightly diverse forms, likewise helps to provide cohesion, especially when such expressions occur both at the beginning and at the end of a unit.

The relationship of a text to the participants in the communication may be regarded as an aspect of intentionality. These relationships can best be described on the basis of what have traditionally been called the functions of a communication: expressive, cognitive, egocentric, informative, imperative, performative, emotive, and phatic. In expressive communication the source is not concerned with the reaction or response of receptors; rather, the source is only concerned with expressing feelings or attitudes typical of "singing in the bathtub" or writing poems that one never expects or hopes that anyone else will read.

The cognitive function of communication is typical of so-called "inner speech", in which the source acts as its own receptor in formulating a discourse so as to more satisfactorily clarify the relationship of certain concepts.

The egocentric function of communication is one in which there is a minimum of information but a maximum effort to call attention to one's own intelligence, knowledge, or verbal fluency.

Informative communication is obviously designed to influence the cognitive state of receptors, while imperative communication seeks to influence the behavior of receptors, and performative communication (illustrated by such a statement as 'I now pronounce you man and wife') certainly changes the status of receptors.

Emotive communication is designed to influence the emotive state of receptors, usually while providing a minimum of information, typical of political speeches and arm-waving of oratory. Phatic communication often contains even less information, but it is designed to reassure the participants of the constant involvement of both source and receptor in the communication act.

In order to perform all of these functions effectively with both impact and appeal (with the corresponding "hitting" and "drawing"), there are two major dimensions: familiar/novel and ugly/beautiful. Familiar rhetorical features obviously serve the purpose of identification, so that receptors are able to identify more effectively with both the message and the source. Novel features, on the other hand, provide impact by virtue of their unpredictability. The dimension of ugly/beautiful is also stylistically significant, for it is possible to employ cacophonous sounds in order to suggest disagreeable content, while esthetically beautiful forms attract receptors to the message.

Various rhetorical features become highly significant in contributing to the effectiveness of various communicative functions. Fresh, figurative language is especially important in providing impact, and parallelism may be particularly appropriate as an esthetic device. Plays on the meanings of related words can be strategic in the cognitive function of language, and shifts in word order can contribute considerably to the imperative aspect of a discourse.

The relationship of a text to the setting, including time, place, and type of audience, depends primarily upon the degree of rhetorical elaboration and upon the language register, which is based essentially upon the degree to which the participants in a communication are known to one another and are in familiar or unfamiliar settings. An elaborate style may be quite appropriate for a sermon, a formal lecture, or a legal defense, but it certainly would be out of place in conversation around the dinner table or chatting at a party. The use of elaborate rhetorical features such as chiasm, strings of near synonyms, complex metaphors, and unusual word order may seem all right in a eulogy, though they may strike many receptors as being artificial, but such features in a prayer may suggest to an audience that the words are directed to the congregation rather than to God, who hardly needs elaborate rhetoric in order to understand the thoughts and meanings of the human heart.

Whether one uses frozen (ritualized), formal, informal, casual, or intimate registers of language depends largely upon the extent to which the persons and the place of a communication are familiar. Frozen language is typical of a baptismal ceremony and a wedding, but it becomes both artificial and boring in a sermon or lecture. Rhetorical features typical of the formal register of language are quite appropriate for someone who is lecturing to people whom he does not know, but for a lecturer to maintain a strictly formal register of language day after day tends to place a psychological barrier between the source and receptors. While informal language may be perfectly appropriate in an office setting, the same persons meeting together at a party are very likely to lapse into a casual level of language, but among members of a family, even the casual level of language is often inappropriate, especially for personal and intimate communication. While the use of anacolutha and minor sentence types (sentence fragments) seems quite out of place in a formal discourse, they are both expected and can be greatly appreciated on a casual or intimate level of communication. When participants in a communication know one another well, it is not necessary to spell out all the details in complete sentences. Accordingly, omissions are not only appropriate, but they also serve to signal the degree of interpersonal identification.

The relationship of a text to the real world may be regarded as essentially a matter of coherence, but coherence must be defined in terms of three important dimensions: real/unreal, factive/fictive, and true/untrue. At first glance, this triple set of distinctions may seem unnecessary, particularly for persons who use the contrast 'true' versus 'untrue' to cover all of these dimensions in various but ambiguous ways. The dimension of real versus unreal (which is, of course, a continuum and not a strict dichotomy) relates to the manner in which the discourse appears to reflect the world which we know or some other world of an author's imagination. People may differ as to the extent to which they regard the Gospel accounts as reflecting the real world, but there is no doubt that the Book of the Apocalypse represents an essentially unreal world. Realism, however, is not merely a matter of something being factive or fictive. Furthermore, the contrast between real and unreal may involve certain aspects of a discourse, but not others. For example, in Kafka's novel The Castle, the microlevel discourses are intensely realistic, but the relationships between episodes are like a dream, and thus in terms of coherence to the world which we know, the macrolevel relations are unreal.

The contrast between factive and fictive deals with literal

historicity. However, a fictive account may closely parallel the events of the real world, and a factive account may give the impression of being unreal.

The contrast between true and untrue (which is likewise in certain respects a continuum) must be dealt with in terms of the level at which a discourse may make a truth claim. The story of the prodigal son, for example, is real in its coherence to the world which we know, but it is fictive in that it did not specifically occur in history. However, it certainly makes a truth claim on several levels. In a sense it is more true to life and contains more truth about the issues of repentance and forgiveness than many expository discourses. Whether one regards a discourse as true or untrue depends, of course, upon one's cultural or intellectual perspective. For Kafka, The Castle is eminently true because of the very absurdity and unreality of the macrolevels in the relations between episodes, since Kafka believed that existence is absurd. The classification of biblical discourses likewise depends upon one's theological preconceptions. For many persons the book of Jonah is real, factive, and true, while for others it is unreal, fictive, but also true, though the elements in the account which make a truth claim may be thought to differ considerably.

The relationship of a text to other texts (intertextuality) involves matters of content and structure. A text may, for example, reproduce some of the content of another text, either by direct quotation or by evident allusion. A person may, of course, conceal the degree of dependency in content and thus be guilty of plagiarism, or one may mimic the content as well as the form of an original in a humorous or satirical way and in so doing produce a parody.

Intertextuality involving structures is in many respects more important than duplications of content, and it is also far more subtle. The principal way in which intertextuality

influences the acceptability of a text derives from the ex-
pectations which people acquire as the result of a degree of
familiarity with the various ways in which discourses can be
organized. There are a relatively limited number of basic
ways in which discourses can be structured. These depend
primarily upon the nature of objects and events in the referential world and upon the stream of consciousness of subjective experience, resulting often in what might be called
a tangential set of relationships between parts of a text.

Discourse structures based upon the stream of consciousness
may provide overt links for a series of statements or the
text may be without such links. In the New Testament the
Johannine writings are particularly good illustrations of
the so-called "stream of consciousness" organization, and
the introductory section of the Gospel of John is an excel-
lent illustration of this type of semantically linked structure, in which the comment element of the first clause or
sentence becomes the topic element of the following clause
or sentence. Note the pairs λόγος...λόγος, θεόν...θεός,
ἐγένετο οὐδὲ ἕν. ὃ γέγονεν, ζωή...ζωή, φῶς...φῶς, σκοτία...
σκοτία. In the writings of James Joyce and a number of
other avant-garde writers the semantic links in the stream
of consciousness are often purposely omitted.

Readers do, however, develop a very significant rhetorical
competence. They readily sense whether the rhetorical
features of a particular discourse are well organized or
not, and they readily react to varying degrees of rhetorical elaboration. It may be difficult for many people to
identify precisely the reasons for approval or disapproval
of a text, but one cannot deny the fact that such judgements
are constantly made and normally on the basis of readily
analyzable factors.

In view of the fact that rhetorical structures involve so
many different types of features which may be arranged in

quite different orders and with different frequencies of occurrence, it is not at all strange that certain distinctive styles result from the variety and density of various rhetorical features. As already noted, the Greek rhetorician Demetrius recognized primarily four major styles. The plain style was primarily neutral in the degree of markedness, but one could not say that the plain style was simply no style at all. It is not a lack of style but a particular choice of style having relatively few rhetorically marked features.

Another style recognized by Hellenistic rhetoricians was the forceful style, which depended greatly upon emphasis and novelty to provide impact. Considerable use was made of repetition, logical relations, and conciseness so as to highlight concern for both the subject matter and the response of readers.

The elaborate style was employed primarily to impress readers with certain formal features. It made use of numerous esthetic devices but was regarded by some persons as being artificial and lacking in genuineness of intent.

The elegant style was designed to match the importance of the content with an appropriate attention to those rhetorical features which would fit lofty concepts. Its purpose was essentially not to attract attention to the rhetorical form but to the relevance of the message.

In the New Testament there are marked differences of style. The fast-moving plain style of Mark certainly contrasts with the more polished and rhetorically organized style of Luke. The syntactically simple but semantically complex style of John is very different from what one finds in Matthew. The Pauline Epistles of Romans and Galatians may be characterized as forceful epistolary style with well-argued logical relations, while the style of the Epistle of James is much more like a pastiche of sermon themes. Probably the most elaborately structured rhetorical features are to be found in the Epistle of 1 Peter, though numerous, elaborate rhetorical forms are also to be found in the Epistle to the Hebrews and especially in 2 Corinthians 10. The Book of Revelation has its own distinctive style, involving not only simple but sometimes crude syntax but with highly complex, symbolic language.

It is comparatively much easier to describe the form of different rhetorical features than to determine their semiotic significance, that is to say, the manner in which they function as signs. The semiotic significance of any rhetorical feature depends upon the system of which the various signs are a part. Such a system is a type of cultural artifact. This means that it is subject to change from time to time. This was true, for example, of the attitude of ancient Greeks concerning plain and elaborated styles. As already noted, the elaborated or elegant styles were particularly appreciated in the early classical period. Later, however, far greater importance was given to the plain or forceful style. In post-New Testament times, however, the pendulum swung back again to the elaborated or elegant styles.

The same type of style can, however, be subject to quite different interpretations. For example, a number of church fathers heavily criticized the plain style of the Greek New Testament for its lack of polished rhetorical structures, while other church fathers praised this fact and emphasized its straightforward, clear structures which paid no homage to human wisdom.

As in the case of lexical and syntactic meanings, rhetorical meanings can likewise be judged both objectively and subjectively, that is to say, in terms of denotation and connotation. Rhetorical features as signs may be judged objectively in the way in which they serve to signal certain relations. For example, in the case of cohesion, features such as repetition, explicit connectives, and parallelism, particularly on a propositional level, are all important signs of textual cohesion. For various aspects of intentionality, those rhetorical features which are prominent in imperative discourse would certainly not fit in expressive discourse, while for performative discourse so-called frozen or ritualized rhetorical devices are common.

In addition to determining more or less objective ways in which rhetorical features are signs of various structural relations in discourse, it is also important to analyze the role of such signs on a subjective level. It is important to know how, and the extent to which, such signs contribute to the impact and appeal of a particular discourse. Impact itself, however, involves complex reactions, for while highly figurative language may have a considerable impact upon one's cognitive appreciation, such figurative expressions may have little effect in terms of behavioral response. The number and arrangement of rhetorical features are, however, highly important for many people in terms of acceptability, as judged by the extent to which such a text properly adheres to the standards which people expect in a particular genre. Rhetorical features relating to coherence and intertextuality seem to be particularly important in contributing to subjective evaluations.

In trying to analyze the way in which rhetorical features function as signs in a semiotic system, one must recognize certain special problems. It may be difficult to determine the specific contribution of a single sign to a discourse, but the variety of signs and the density of these features make possible a far more relevant analysis. This is not strange, for it parallels in certain ways what one experiences on a lexical level. Determining the meaning of lexical units by defining them on the basis of the range of potential referents based on the bundle of distinctive features is relatively difficult. In fact, it is much easier usually to state the meaning of a sentence, for the various lexical units in a sentence delimit the semantic range of the individual lexical signs. Parallelism as a rhetorical feature may be a sign of a number of different relations, and it is difficult in some instances to specify the manner in which such a feature marks a discourse. However, a combination of several juxtaposed parallel expressions plus a number of figurative meanings usually constitute a clear sign of liturgical/poetic discourse.

CHAPTER 3

Types of Texts

Without knowing the type of text involved, one might well
assume that the statement "the islanders slaughtered the
rangers" refers to some savage murders on some remote island, but on the sports page of The New York Times this refers to the lopsided results in a game played by two hockey
teams in the eastern part of the United States. Similarly,
the statement "I had thirty yards of daylight in front of
me" seems strange, but as a statement by an American foot-
ball player who had just received a pass, the obvious meaning was that there was nothing to stop the player from
rushing headlong to the goal line. Since these two statements are typical of texts produced by sportswriters, one
soon recognizes the meaning, but without an awareness of the
discourse genre, both confusion and misinterpretation readily result.

The type of text (or discourse genre) always contributes
significantly to the meaning of a discourse, for it provides
important clues as to interpretation. In other words, the
type of text itself constitutes a sign, and readers readily
recognize the significance of text types, even though it may
be difficult to define precisely the significance of such
literary forms. A text type may function as a sign only
because there is a system of text types. The contrasts and
similarities between such texts provide the basis for the
semiotic significance of the various sorts of texts. Even
the format in which a text is presented may constitute a
significant signal as to the way in which the text is to be
understood. Compare, for example, the following two paragraphs:
Format A:
After years of stock car racing, running rifles to Cuba,
money from Rio, high diving from helicopters into the Gulf;

after life at gunpoint, on the dare, my father can't make the trip out of Miami.

Format B:

> After years of stock car racing, running
> rifles to Cuba, money from Rio, high
> diving from helicopters into the Gulf;
> after life at gunpoint, on the dare,
> my father can't make the trip out of Miami.

In format A one immediately assumes that this is simply an introductory statement or brief paragraph for a prose account, evidently about some man's difficulties in overcoming fear at an advanced age despite his earlier daredevil existence.

With format B the situation changes considerably. The content is the same, and yet the poetic format suggests that there is more involved in this statement, something deeper, something more universal, something perhaps more important.

Actually format B is the correct reproduction of the first paragraph of a poem by Daniel Mark Epstein entitled "Miami" and printed on page 202 of The American Scholar for the Spring, 1982.

Or, compare the following paragraphs in two different formats:

Format A:

If the mugger in our mind represents the fear of violence and early death, modern life has added yet another fear to the arsenal of human horrors -- that of living too long.

Format B:

>If the mugger in our mind
>represents the fear
>of violence and early death,
>modern life has added
>yet another fear
>to the arsenal of human horrors --
>that of living too long.

The first format suggests a striking theme of an essay on modern life, and we could well imagine that this would introduce a series of statements concerning the problems of aging, but format B suggests that we should look deeper into this statement, especially in view of such phrases as "the mugger in our mind", "violence and early death", and "the arsenal of human horrors". In fact, the final line suggests that this may very well be a complete poem in which unwarranted fear expressed by "the mugger in our mind" is to be related somehow to this tragedy of "living too long".

Actually, however, format A is the form of this statement, which occurs in an essay titled "Has the Future a Future?" also published in The American Scholar, page 160, for Spring, 1982.

In the ancient Greco-Roman world, the principal text types were epic poetry, lyric poetry, dramatic poetry (drama), biography, history, letters (both personal and public), speeches, laws, official notices, epigrams, and essays. Some of the more typically embedded text types were parables, allegories, proverbs, and riddles. In the modern world there are a number of additional text types, including novels, short stories, minutes of proceedings, conversations, recipes (and how-to-do-it manuals), and jokes. Some classical literary genres have lost much of their popularity and attractiveness. Epic poetry is rarely attempted in the modern western world, and drama is normally in the form of prose rather than poetry.

For the New Testament the principal text types are dramatic history, letters, and apocalyptic. The dramatic history may be either focused upon an individual (in which case it may be regarded as primarily biographical, as in the case of the Gospels) or historical, as in the case of the Acts of the Apostles, though some have insisted that one might better speak of "the Acts of the Holy Spirit".

The letters are of three principal classes: personal, to a particular constituency, and general. The letter to Philemon is probably the only strictly personal letter, but the letters 1 and 2 Timothy and Titus may be regarded as semipersonal, at least in formal structure. The letters from Romans through 2 Thessalonians are addressed, at least formally, to particular constituencies, and they deal with a number of theological and practical issues. Scholars have, however, raised questions concerning the letter to the Ephesians, since it seems to be of a more general character. The textual problem in Ephesians 1.1 also lends support to this view.

The Epistle to the Hebrews is a type of literary hybrid, in that in content it is more like an essay, though the ending (Hebrews 13.20-24) employs a typical epistolary benediction and greeting, despite the fact that there is no corresponding introductory salutation.

The General Letters, James through Jude, are for the most part directed to a much wider audience, and the contents consist of general admonitions rather than responses to specific issues or problems. 2 and 3 John may be regarded as either personal or as directed to a particular constituency; this depends largely upon the interpretation of the introductory paragraph.

The apocalyptic text type is distinct in its heavy symbolism, its veiled allusions, and its involved series of sequences reflecting temporal and spatial relations.

The primary embedded text types in the New Testament consist of miracle stories, parables, allegories, conversations, speeches (teaching, sermons, legal pleas), liturgical fragments (usually typical of Hebrew poetic structure), and quotations.

Many of the miracle stories are more than mere accounts of some miraculous event. They are regarded by some as "pronouncement texts", since the miracle is related to some concluding pronouncement which indicates the significance of the event. This is particularly true of the miracles recorded in the Gospel of John, since all of these miracles are spoken of as "signs".

Though present-day scholars have tried to make a clear distinction between parables (stories with a single significant point) and allegories (in which each detail of a story usually has some corresponding relationship to something else), this distinction is hard to maintain in the New Testament. It is true that in a number of instances the explanation of a parable turns it into a type of allegory, as, for example, in the case of the parable of the weeds among the wheat (Matthew 13.24-30, 36-43). In the New Testament itself, only the term "parable" is used for all such stories, and even for more or less epigrammatic sayings.

Speeches in the New Testament are essentially of three types: teaching (sometimes with various topics grouped together, as in the case of the Sermon on the Mount), sermons, and legal pleas, whether in the case of Tertullus (Acts 24.2b-9) or Paul's defense (Acts 24.10b-21). The liturgical embedded texts in the New Testament are essentially of three types: (1) songs or expressions of praise, e.g. Luke 1.47-55 and 1.68-79, (2) prayers, e.g. the so-called "Lord's Prayer" (Matthew 6.9-13),[11] and (3) confessions of faith, e.g. Philippians 2.6-11 and 1 Timothy 3.16. The liturgical form of this confession in 1 Timothy 3.16 seems quite clear, especially when it is rendered in a format which focuses upon the balance of certain lines, as already noted in chapter two.

It is possible to treat so-called "conversations" in the New Testament as simply a matter of teaching an individual, but quite clearly the literary form of a conversation has a distinct structure. This is particularly true in some of the conversations in the Gospel of John. In John 3 (the conversation with Nicodemus) and in John 4 (the conversation with the woman of Samaria), the rhetorical structure is very similar. After certain introductory and largely phatic statements, Jesus makes an ambiguous and enigmatic declaration which is immediately misinterpreted in a strictly literal or physical sense rather than in a figurative or spiritual sense. Jesus responds, but his explanation is not fully comprehended. This then leads to an extended explanation in which the spiritual significance of the misunderstood declaration is explained and elaborated upon.

The quotations in the New Testament are clearly of two types: (a) popular sayings from an oral tradition and (b) quotations of specific texts. Some appear to be merely quotations of popular sayings, for example, "for where your treasure is, there is your heart" (Matthew 6.21) or "you

---

11   Though John 17 has the literary form of a prayer, in that the words are formally addressed to God, the content is essentially a brief essay on the oneness of Christ with the Father and the oneness of Christ with his disciples and future believers. Strictly as a prayer, one might say that it tends to violate a discourse maxim, namely, not saying to a receptor something which is already fully known.

cannot serve God and mammon" (Matthew 6.24) or "but new wine is put into new wineskins" (Mark 2.22). The numerous quotations of specific texts come primarily from the Septuagint Greek text, which was the "Bible" of the church of the first century. A quotation from a secular source occurs in Acts 17.28 "for we are his offspring".

In addition to specific quotations in which one must assume that the author had in mind a particular text, the New Testament has a number of literary allusions. Mary's song of praise in Luke 1.47-55 is full of phrases which are similar to those in passages of the Old Testament. The same is even more true of Zechariah's prophetic utterance in Luke 1.68-79.

One text type in which there are striking differences between present-day usage and that which is recorded in the New Testament is to be found in the form of speeches. At the present time, speeches are relatively long (often thirty minutes to an hour, or even longer). They are oral, even though a person may follow a written text; the form is prose; and the style may range from frozen (or ritual) to informal. Almost any topic may be the subject matter of a speech, but there may be great differences in the extent or relevance of the content. Political speeches often aim primarily at emotive identification with the speaker rather than content (too many promises can haunt politicians). Similarly, many sermons are designed to stir the emotions so that people will respond to the admonitions rather than being impressed with the nature of the Good News. In the literary form in which a speech is printed, either the speech is given in full or the text indicates clearly that the material consists of excerpts.

In the case of speeches in the New Testament, there is no indication whatsoever that persons spoke from a written manuscript. Far too much attention was paid to rhetorical

skill and oratory in the schools of ancient Greece and Rome
for such a practice to have been developed or approved.
What does occur, however, in the New Testament is that the
speeches are given in summary form, following the practice
of Thucydides, which he illustrated magnificently and
defended as the right of a historian to provide the gist of
a speech, both in terms of its content and emotive mode.

The New Testament also exhibits composite speeches, as in
the case of the Sermon on the Mount, in which it would appear that various utterances of Jesus made at different
times and at different places are gathered together in a
structured form. Naturally Jesus would have repeated many
parables on different occasions and developed various themes
in slightly different ways, depending upon the audience and
the setting, but the way in which these are presented in the
New Testament is completely typical of the method approved
of in ancient times for recording such utterances.

A text type which is almost the complete opposite of a rhetorically well formed speech would be the text of a telegram. In both the speech and telegram the structure is
prose, not poetry, but a telegram tends to be short, syntactically elliptical, with words often substituting for
crucial marks of punctuation (some persons might even object
to calling the texts of telegrams a "text type"). Telegrams
normally do not reflect literary rhetorical devices, but one
cannot discuss text types without taking into consideration
the total range of possibilities.

It is often much easier to describe various text types than
it is to define them, especially if one attempts to do so in
terms of "necessary and sufficient features". Such definitions often become highly problematic because of a tendency
for overlapping and cases of mixed text types. It is far
better to describe such text types in terms of "a family of
features", many of which may be optional. Furthermore, one

must also reckon with various gradations in such features. Normally one thinks of a novel as being significantly longer than a short story, but length is also subject to gradation, so that one may have a short novel and a long short story, and there is really no clear-cut distinction based merely upon length.

The greatest controversies with regard to text types have centered on the issue of prose versus poetry. Up to the end of the nineteenth century there was very little controversy on this issue, since poetry was often defined in terms of meter and rhyme, especially if one was considering various European languages, but all of this has been changed in the twentieth century. In the first place, a great deal of free verse has been written in the languages of western Europe. Rhyme has been largely abandoned, and meter is subject to all kinds of internal variations. Studies in the literature of other languages of the world have shown that meter in the sense of accented feet as the constituent elements of mea-sured lines is by no means universal. The measurement of such lines may be based upon stressed syllables, length of vowels, length of syllables, number of syllables, number of words, etc. Literary analysts have therefore had to rethink many of their preconceptions with regard to the nature of poetry. This has been particularly helpful in terms of the analysis of poetic structures in the New Testament, since these are based so largely upon Hebrew, which likewise does not make use of meter or of rhyme but does have a number of features typical of poetic texts in many different languages.

Hebrew poetry does have a feature of what might be called "measured lines", in that generally the overall length of related lines is roughly similar. One of the most conspi-cuous features of Hebrew poetry, however, is the condensa-tion of the meaning, that is to say, there is a good deal of semantic ellipsis so that the text does not spell out all of

the possibly relevant background information but aims at
succinct and striking ways of relating similar or antithetical expressions. Hebrew poetry also makes great use of
figurative language, and though the syntax is often quite
simple, the semotaxis is highly complex, that is to say, the
relations between juxtaposed expressions are often quite unusual.

The use of figurative language and complex semotaxis usually
implies multiple levels of meaning, not necessarily based
upon calculated obscurity or ambiguity but upon the use of
symbolic archetypes such as life/death, love/hate, right/
wrong, and goodness/evil.

As Kugel (1981) has pointed out, even the distinction between "prose" and "poetry" in the Hebrew texts of the Old
Testament is essentially artificial. This is especially
true of the writings of the prophets, in which there is often an almost imperceptible gradation between what would be
called prose narrative and poetic parallelism. In fact, it
is often not possible to determine whether a particular
passage in Hebrew should be printed in poetic format or
simply in prose paragraph style.

Roman Jakobson (1960) has made a number of insightful com-
ments concerning poetry as being essentially based upon
parallelism. Metrical arrangements, whether based upon
length of vowels, length of syllables, number of syllables,
or number of words, are essentially matters of parallelism,
since corresponding lines involve repeated patterns of such
metrical arrangements. The occurrence of certain sounds,
whether onomatopoeic representations, assonance or alliteration, or rhyme, are likewise matters of parallelism. On
the lexical level the repetition of words or themes may
likewise be regarded as instances of parallelism, and even
figurative expressions are in a sense semantic parallels
between literal and extended meanings. The fact that on a

propositional level poetry makes use of extended figures, even to the point of incorporating parables and allegories, may likewise be considered as features of parallelism.

But far more important than the features of so-called poetic discourse is the function of poetry. As a sociosemiotic sign, what significance does poetry have? How does it influence the interpretation of a text? What does the poetic structure actually contribute to the meaning of such a discourse? For the Bible there are five important contributions which poetic structure makes to a text. In the first place, it highlights and emphasizes the significance of the theme. The very unusualness of the structure adds impact and therefore calls attention to the lexical content. In the second place, poetic structure no doubt makes passages more esthetically attractive. The balance, symmetry, and rhythm of such texts makes them more pleasurable. In the third place, the use of poetic structures permits the grouping of ideas in ways which defy normal logical formulations but which expressed important insights and relations which people can feel but not necessarily explain. In the fourth place, the use of poetic structure immediately identifies a passage as having some supernatural basis or implication. Since God was not supposed to speak in precisely the same manner as humans, it was not at all strange that poetic utterances in the Bible were associated with the declarations of deity and with utterances having important theological implications. Not only did God speak through the prophets in poetic form, but the same type of poetic structure would be appropriate for persons addressing God, so that both prophecy and prayer constituted proper cases for poetic utterance. In the fifth place, poetic structures provide a high degree of emotive impact, something which the Greek rhetoricians fully recognized and appreciated. But in the Bible the emotive impact is even more enhanced by the association of poetic features with divine authority.

Since diverse text types exist in all literate cultures, one might very well inquire as to what is the real value of such different literary genres. First, they no doubt constitute important models to be followed by writers or speakers who wish to communicate particular kinds of messages to various types of audiences under special circumstances. The existence of such models certainly provides a source with a convenient structure which can be followed in such a way as to be both effective and acceptable.

Second, the existence of such text types as models for communication serves to facilitate decoding on the part of those who receive the message, whether orally or in written form. Being familiar with a particular genre greatly assists in the process of understanding the meaning and significance of a text. For example, understanding the book of Revelation would have been almost impossible for the early Christian church unless these persons had been familiar with the apocalyptic symbolism in the book of Daniel, the prophecies of Ezekiel, and other popular apocalyptic writings of that time. Without the benefit of insights from other related texts, one could grievously misinterpret apocalyptic literature, something which unfortunately occurs extensively even in our own day, since many people want to interpret apocalyptic literature in a strictly literal, rather than in a symbolic, sense.

Third, the existence of various text types also provides important frameworks for remembering content. As soon as a receptor has identified the basic text type of any utterance, the relevant elements of the content are grasped largely in terms of such a framework. The familiar structure of such a text type thus provides a series of "pigeon holes" into which information can be mentally filed.

Though it is true that certain literary genres lend themselves more readily to particular kinds of content, it would be quite wrong to think that for any one idea only one corresponding genre is appropriate. In order to deal with the dynamic tension in the issues of love and hate, one may employ any one of a number of different text types, for example, a story, an illustrative historical event, a parable, a poem, or a proverb. Each text type would add its own significant dimension to such a theme.

CHAPTER 4

The Meaning of Lexical Units

In this volume meaning is understood in a broad sense, that is, in terms of the semiotic significance of any unit or structure which serves as a sign of something. As already noted in Chapters 2 and 3, individual rhetorical features or groupings of such features as distinctive elements of literary genres have semiotic significance and hence meaning in the sense employed here. It is, however, essential to analyze somewhat more fully the meaning of those linguistic units which consist essentially of lexical features, that is to say, words. Such units may involve individual bound morphemes, single words, idioms, and typically embedded statements (proverbs, adages), and complete discourses. One special aspect of lexical meaning, namely, the symbolic significance of referents, is reserved for Chapter 5 and combinatory meaning is treated in Chapters 6 and 7.

In order to appreciate fully the contribution of lexical units to the meaning of discourse, it is essential to study these problems from a number of perspectives: (1) the distinction between meaning and reference, (2) the problem of multiple meanings of lexical units, (3) the distinction between literal and figurative meanings, (4) the problems associated with idioms, (5) semantic classes, (6) the structures of related meanings and (7) the meaning of larger discourse units.

Meaning and Reference

In dealing with the meaning of lexical units, one of the most difficult distinctions to bear in mind is the significant difference between meaning and reference. It may be useful, in fact, to highlight the difference by speaking of "conceptual/denotative meaning" (often thought of as "dictionary meaning") and "discourse reference", since in distinguishing between meaning and reference we are concerned essentially with the difference between a dictionary defini- tion of a particular meaning and the range of reference which such a term may have in a variety of contexts. For example, a definition of the meaning of <u>chair</u> may be stated as a "piece of furniture employed as a seat for one person and having a back, and being moveable". In this way, the meaning of <u>chair</u> is distinguished from the meanings of <u>bench</u>, <u>stool</u>, and <u>sofa</u>. This term <u>chair</u> can be used in speaking of hundreds of different shapes and sizes of chairs, including those with arms or without arms, made of quite different materials (wood, metal, plastic, etc.), of quite different heights, and with varying types of ornamen- tation. The meaning of <u>chair</u> consists of those distinctive features which make possible the use of such a term in designating a wide variety of referents. In a similar way, the Greek term θήκη, which occurs in John 18.11 and there refers to a sheath for a sword, also occurs in Greek to refer to a chest, coffin, tomb, or quiver. Under such cir- cumstances, is one to set up a number of different meanings for θήκη on the basis of each different type of referent, or is the meaning of θήκη simply "a container appropriate for the safe storage of a variety of objects"? Such a defini- tion of θηκη involves abstracting from the range of refe- rents those features which make possible the use of θήκη in a relatively generic sense.

The verb αἰτέω occurs in a number of different types of con- texts. One may, for example, ask for a fish (Matthew 7.10) or ask for a sign (1 Corinthians 1.22). One may also ask for alms (Acts 3.2) or a favor (Acts 25.3) or ask for some- thing from God (Mark 11.24). It is also possible to ask for an accounting, and in such a context one might very well translate 'demand'. One might wish to translate αἰτέω by a number of different words in English, depending upon the context, for example, 'to ask for', 'to pray', 'to beg', 'to demand'. These would be perfectly appropriate referents in various contexts, but the dictionary meaning of αἰτέω can perhaps be more precisely stated as 'to ask for on the basis of presumed need'. This would imply both legitimacy and urgency of the request. But within a particular context, for example, when one is 'asking something from God', it would be perfectly appropriate to speak of the reference as 'to pray'. Depending upon the degree of urgency, one might very well also translate αἰτέω as 'to beg', but this does not mean that αἰτέω has a number of different meanings. It is only that the meaning of αἰτέω is such as to make possible the use of the term in a number of different contexts in which there are different referents.

Multiple Meanings

There is a somewhat different problem involved in treating multiple meanings of a lexical unit. πνεῦμα, for example, may mean 'wind', 'breath', 'inner being' (in contrast with σάρξ 'flesh' and σῶμα 'body'), 'a non-physical independent being', and 'the Holy Spirit'. One might very well ask why in the case of αἰτέω the seeming variety of senses or referents is combined into a single dictionary meaning, while in the case of πνεῦμα a number of different meanings are postulated. For one thing, all of the different referents of αἰτέω can be combined readily within the same semantic domain involving communication, but in the case of the various meanings of πνεῦμα, this is not possible. The meaning of 'wind' obviously belongs in a domain of physical events, while 'breath' is an aspect of physiological events. The meaning of πνεῦμα as 'inner being' belongs to the domain of human personality. It is true that the meaning of 'non-physical entity' is related to the meaning of 'Holy Spirit', but these are again related to one another in terms of generic and specific.

An even more obvious case of distinctions in meaning is to be found with the Greek term σάρξ, which in 2 Corinthians 7.5 refers to the physical nature or state of a person, and

in Romans 11.14, to a particular ethnic group. In Acts
2.17, σάρξ refers to people in general and in Romans 8.3 to
human nature. It might be possible to formulate some highly
generic expression which would in some way link together
these various meanings, but any such formulation would be so
abstract as to be semantically useless. Since these various
meanings of σάρξ relate to quite distinct semantic domains
and involve very different sets of distinctive features, it
is far more satisfactory to recognize the existence of a
variety of meanings. No doubt some of these differences in
meaning were originally regarded as figurative, but the
usage became so conventionalized that in the employment of
the term σάρξ in such different contexts Greek speakers
would not be aware of both the literal and the extended
meanings but would simply reckon with one of the multiple
meanings of σάρξ. The existence of multiple meanings of the
same word is common in all languages. For example, in
English one may readily use the term bar in speaking of a
bar on the door, a bar at the mouth of a river, a bar of
gold, a bar as a place to drink, and the bar as a legal
institution. Though historically these meanings are all
related, most speakers of English would use them without any
significant awareness of the relations between the meanings.

Wherever there is an evident play on the distinct referents
of a word, one may be certain that there is a distinction in
meaning. For example, in John 3.8 πνεῦμα is clearly used in
two quite distinct senses, 'wind' and 'Spirit'. Similarly,
in John 3.3 ἄνωθεν may mean 'again' or 'from above', in
which case the first meaning belongs to the domain of time
and the second meaning to the domain of space.

Figurative Meanings
As already noted in the analysis of multiple meanings, one
must also be concerned with the distinction between literal
and figurative meanings. The literal meaning of a word may
be best regarded as the "unmarked meaning of a term", that

is to say, it would be the meaning which people would associate with such a term when the supporting context is minimal. This usually occurs when a word is used in isolation
and without any so-called "defining context". For example,
the Greek term ὄνομα in isolation is normally understood as
'name', but in a context such as 'to believe in the name of
Christ', ὄνομα no longer designates merely a 'name' but
a 'person', namely, Christ. Similarly, in isolation γόνυ is
understood as meaning 'knee', but in the expression ἐμοὶ
κάμψει πᾶν γόνυ 'every knee shall bow to me' (Romans 14.11)
the meaning of γόνυ is not 'knee' but 'person'.

In the use of ὄνομα and γόνυ in the sense of 'person' rather
than 'name' or 'knee', respectively, there is a clear relationship between the part and the whole, that is to say,
between the 'name' and the 'knee' as a part of a person and
the person as an organic unit. This relationship also seems
to have a certain amount of psychological relevance or
force. It is this implied relationship which justifies
one's dealing with such meanings as being figurative in contrast with literal.

In Matthew 5.14, ὑμεῖς ἐστε τὸ φῶς τοῦ κόσμου 'you are the
light of the world', φῶς must obviously be understood in a
figurative sense, for people are never literally 'light'.
Similarly, in John 1.12 τέκνα 'children' in the phrase τέκνα
θεοῦ, literally 'children of God', must be understood
figuratively, since those who receive God have not been
literally engendered by God but simply have come into a new
relationship to God.

It is not always possible to determine the extent to which a
meaning is to be regarded simply as one of the multiple
literal meanings of a word or whether it is better treated
as a figurative extension of meaning on the basis that there
is some significant awareness of the relationship between
the literal and the extended sense. For example, the Greek

term καρπός, literally 'fruit', is also widely used in the sense of 'result, outcome, product'. However, in the case of the phrase καρπὸν δικαιοσύνης 'the product of righteousness' (Philippians 1.11) it is doubtful that the Greek reader would be aware of this figurative relationship. In English the verb <u>conceive</u> may mean 'to become pregnant' or 'to intellectually formulate some idea', but it would be rare indeed for an English-speaking person to use the second meaning with a conscious awareness of the first.

In many instances it is important to reckon with a distinction between widely used and conventionalized figurative meanings and those which seem to be innovative and perhaps even unique. For example, in John 6.53 the statement ἐὰν μὴ φάγητε τὴν σάρκα τοῦ υἱοῦ τοῦ ἀνθρώπου καὶ πίητε αὐτοῦ τὸ αἷμα, οὐκ ἔχετε ζωὴν ἐν ἑαυτοῖς 'if you do not eat the flesh of the Son of Man and drink his blood, you do not have life in yourselves' must be understood in a highly figurative sense, but this seems not to have been a well-established figurative meaning in Hellenistic Greek, but an innovative figurative usage. The same may be true of πανοπλίαν 'complete armor' in Ephesians 6.13 and ἐκένωσεν 'emptying' in Philippians 2.7.

Since figurative meanings tend to be so culturally specific, one must always be aware of the fact that in other languages the closest corresponding terms may have quite different figurative meanings. It seems to make perfectly good sense to say in English 'though your sins be as scarlet, they shall be white as snow' (Isaiah 1.18), but in certain areas of the Orient, scarlet is a symbol of marriage and joy, and white is a symbol of death and mourning.

The Meaning of Idioms

Special problems of figurative meanings are involved in idioms, that is to say, combinations of two or more words which have a meaning which cannot be derived from the meaning of the component parts. The phrase θυγάτηρ Σιών 'daughter of Zion' is particularly complex because normally it means 'Jerusalem', but in John 12.15 it is used figuratively to designate 'the people of Jerusalem'. In Matthew 16.17 the statement σὰρξ καὶ αἷμα οὐκ ἀπεκάλυψέν σοι 'flesh and blood has not revealed it to you' does not make sense if one insists on interpreting σὰρξ καὶ αἷμα in a literal sense. Clearly, this phrase is an idiom meaning 'person as representative of mankind'. A failure to recognize idioms can lead to unfortunate misunderstanding. In 1 Corinthians 13.2 the expression 'faith to remove mountains' must certainly be understood in an idiomatic sense of 'faith such as to do the seemingly impossible', though some people assume it should be understood in a literal sense.

Semantic Classes

An important element in the semantic analysis of lexical units involves the determination of the semantic classes of such units. Basically there are four such classes, which to a certain extent parallel syntactic classes, but which are by no means coterminous with such syntactic classes. The four basic semantic classes are objects (or entities), events and related states, abstracts, and relationals. Meanings belonging to the object class denote such objects (or entities) as man, woman, tree, sun, moon, building, mountain, lake, that is to say, objects with relatively fixed Gestalts (or forms). The class of events and related states involves meanings such as run, walk, think, talk, eat, sleep, fall, die, and such related states as asleep, fallen and dead. Abstracts are essentially of three major types: (1) those referring primarily to features of objects, e.g. red, green, tall, big, (2) those referring primarily to the features of events, e.g. fast, slow, propitious, timely, and (3) those referring to the features of other abstracts (primarily matters of degree), e.g. too, very, exceedingly. Relationals, which are a special type of abstracts, constitute the fourth principal semantic class. They consist of four major classes: (1) those relating to space, e.g. <u>above</u>, <u>below</u>, <u>around</u>, (2) those relating to time, e.g. <u>while</u>, <u>when</u>, <u>during</u>, (3) those relating to the communicative setting (deictics), e.g. <u>this</u>, <u>that</u> (though this class may be regarded as a subtype of spatial relationals), and (4) those relating to logical relations, e.g. <u>because</u>, <u>for</u>, <u>but</u>, <u>or</u>, <u>so that</u>, <u>in order to</u>.

There is an obvious parallelism between semantic classes and syntactic classes, but by no means complete correspondence. For example, in most Indo-European languages it is common to express events by nominalized verbs, and abstracts are frequently expressed by nouns. In many languages, however, numerous abstracts fall into the syntactic class of verbs, and many relationals may be simply possessed nouns.

The meaning of most lexical units can be defined on the basis of sensory input from the respective referents, but for some lexical units meaning must be defined in conceptual terms since there are no observable models which may provide a basis for determining the conceptual content. This is true, for example, of such terms as <u>mermaid</u>, <u>unicorn</u>, <u>trinity</u>, and <u>God</u>.

If the meaning of a lexical unit belongs to only one major semantic class, the problem of analysis is not too complex. This is true, for example, of terms whose denotation may be regarded as structurally similar to such words as <u>chair</u>, <u>think</u>, <u>red</u>, but when a term belongs to more than one major semantic class, complications immediately arise. For example, in English the term <u>dancer</u> belongs not only to the object class, since it refers to a person, but also to the class of an incorporated event, namely, dancing. The distinction becomes particularly significant in a phrase such as <u>two good dancers</u>, since <u>two</u> qualifies the object semantic element in <u>dancers</u>, while <u>good</u> qualifies the event element. The occurrence of more than one semantic class is, however,

not related merely to morphological complexity. The term
heir involves not only object and event but an abstract of
time and a complex relational, so that one may define heir
as 'one who is to inherit or who has inherited something
upon the death of someone else'. The Greek term ἐπίσκοπος
belongs not only to the object class but indicates an event
and a relationship to someone else and can perhaps be best
defined as 'one who has administrative responsibility for
the care of others'. If one understands δικαιοσύνη in certain Pauline contexts as referring essentially to a covenant
relationship and thus interprets 'the righteousness of God'
in Romans 1.17 as 'the manner in which God puts people right
with himself', there is obviously a very complex semantic
structure involving an event, an abstract of 'rightness' and
a relationship.

Structures of Related Meanings

As already carefully noted in Chapter 1, meanings of lexical
units always occur in structures, that is to say, the meaning of any one lexical sign is defined in terms of what
might be called a mosaic of signs, often consisting of several layers. In a sense, the meanings of any lexical unit
are defined negatively by the presence of other lexical
units in the same semantic domain. The ways in which the
various sets of related meanings define one another by
mutual exclusion are of four basic types: (1) clusters, (2)
hierarchies (or inclusions), (3) overlappings, and (4) con-
trastives.

A typical cluster of meanings is to be found in the subdomain of artifacts specifying a number of weapons, for
example, ῥομφαία 'a large, broad sword used for both cutting
and piercing', μάχαιρα 'a relatively short sword, or even a
dagger, used for cutting and stabbing', λόγχη 'a long weapon
with sharpened end used for piercing by thrusting or as a
projectile by hurling', ὑσσός 'a type of short spear or
javelin', βέλος 'a missile such as an arrow or dart'. Events

may also occur in such clusters. Compare, for example, βαστάζω 'to bear or carry something that is relatively heavy or burdensome' (Mark 14.13), τρέφω 'to carry something back to a point where it had been formerly' (Matthew 27.3), αἴρω 'to lift up and carry away' (Mark 6.29), σύρω 'to drag' (Acts 14.19), ἄγω 'to lead' (Matthew 21.7). In the case of all of these related meanings, one object causes another object to move and in the process both objects move in space.

Hierarchies of meaning involving successive sets of included meanings are common in all languages. A typical series in English would be 'animal', 'canine', 'dog', 'poodle', in which the relationships can be expressed in terms of the fact that all poodles are dogs, all dogs are canines, and all canines are animals. Similar patterns of semantic relations may exist for events, for example, the generic meaning of αἰτέω 'to ask for', may be said to include ἀπαιτέω 'to ask for something back' (Luke 6.30) or ζητέω 'to ask for something which is especially sought, to satisfy a real or presumed need' (Mark 8.11), or δέομαι 'to ask for with a sense of urgency' (Luke 8.28).

The overlapping relationship between meanings is the basis for so-called synonyms. In reality there are probably no two words in any language which have exactly the same meaning, both on a denotative (or designative) and connotative (or associative) level, but in all languages there are words which seem to be so closely related in meaning that they appear to substitute readily for one another, particularly in contexts where stylistic variety seems to be important. In the Greek New Testament this may include such pairs as φιλέω/ἀγαπάω, λόγος/ῥῆμα, and ὁράω/βλέπω.

Contrastive sets of related meanings are of three major types: (1) positive/negative, e.g. ἀγαθός/κακός 'good/bad' on one semantic dimension and ἀγαθός/πονηρός 'good/evil' on another semantic dimension; (2) reversives, e.g. θάνατος/

ἀνάστασις 'death/resurrection'; and (3) reciprocals, e.g.
αἰτέω/λαμβάνω 'ask/receive' and δανείζω/δανείζομαι 'lend/
borrow'.

It is normally not too difficult to determine the different
meanings of the same lexical unit, for different meanings
are usually quite far apart in "semantic space". What is
much more difficult and at the same time far more significant, especially for the rhetorical level of language, is
the determination of the differences in the related meanings
of different lexical units, since these tend to be much closer together in semantic space. In order to distinguish
adequately between related meanings of different words, it
is important to determine the three types of features which
serve to define the differences. First there are the shared
features of meaning which exist for any set of related meanings. These shared features are those which serve to place
such meanings within the same semantic domain or subdomain.
Those features which distinguish between terms within any
such domain or subdomain are the diagnostic (or distinctive)
features. On a purely denotative level of meaning, the
diagnostic features may be relatively clear, as in the case
of the meanings for the various terms for weapons cited
above, but for any lexical unit there are always additional
supplementary features of meaning which are crucial for the
connotations of lexical units. They also normally form the
basis for figurative extensions of meaning. It is easy
enough to determine the popular differences of meaning between pigeon and dove on the basis of the shape of the tail.
This type of information is readily obtainable on the basis
of comparing the referents of the respective terms, but it
is not easy to determine the basis for the supplementary
meaning attached to dove, which makes possible a phrase such
as harmless as a dove. In reality, doves are not peaceful,
harmless birds; in fact, they are well known for their mur-
derous instincts toward other incapacitated doves. The connotative meaning associated with dove is therefore something

which results not from the nature of the referents but from cultural attitudes and opinions with regard to such refe- rents. This is essentially encyclopedic information which is not derivable from a linguistic taxonomy.

Meaning of Larger Discourse Units

In addition to lexical units involving individual words and phrases (idioms), one must also deal with larger discourse units, either embedded or complete.

In Matthew 7.6 the statement about not giving what is holy to dogs nor casting pearls before swine has all the charac- teristics of a proverb or adage, but its interpretation is dependent upon the cultural fact that Jews regarded Gen- tiles as dogs and swine, and therefore one could only under- stand this proverbial saying in terms of not giving that which is holy to Gentiles nor casting valuable objects be- fore such persons.

For proverbial sayings there are often several degrees of decodability. It is easy enough, for example, to interpret the West African proverb "a dry leaf does not laugh when his neighbor falls", since this readily suggests that one should not laugh at the distress of someone else, for one is likely to soon suffer the same fate. But for the Haitian proverb "no one picks up a lightning stone", it is simply impossible to arrive at a correct meaning without knowing a good deal about the cultural context in which ancient pre-Colombian artifacts are called "lightning stones", since they are regarded as having been formed by lightning. Anyone who finds such an object and picks it up immediately obligates himself to becoming a medicine man, which is usually re- garded as a rather dangerous occupation in view of the fact that so many patients do not survive.

To understand a parable it is often necessary to have con- siderable background information so as to reckon satisfactorily with the symbolic significance of various features of the text. In the story of the prodigal son it is certainly important to recognize what is meant for a Jew to work for a foreigner and especially to be engaged in taking care of swine and even wanting to eat the same food that the swine ate. The symbolic importance attached to the garment, shoes, and ring given by the father to the son upon his return is likewise extremely important.

Total discourse units also have meaning. For the primitive church in the second century, the book of Revelation was undoubtedly especially meaningful to the Christian in-group. Although the persecutions were at times extremely threatening and violent, the book provided believers with the assurance of ultimate victory, and it thus gave meaning to suffering and death. The very fact that it was written in esoteric language no doubt heightened its meaning for the people, since it would be understandable only to those acquainted with biblical symbolism, and this undoubtedly assured them that the message was directed particularly to them.

The meaning of any total discourse unit is always more than the sum of the individual parts. For the Gospel of John, there is the drama of increase, decrease, and exultation, though expressed in somewhat greater detail in the four-part drama of acceptance, opposition, defeat, and victory. For the book of Acts the motifs are basically geographic and ethnic, but the overall design is a matter of the expansion of Christian witness by the power of the Holy Spirit in the face of ethno-religious problems which changed the understanding of the church concerning its own nature and purpose.

As already intimated in the discussions of the meanings of lexical units and particularly in the significance of embedded discourses and total discourses, meaning cannot be restricted merely to adding up even the literal or figurative significance of individual words. This is particularly true since words are simply signs of referents which in turn may function as signs of still other referents. It is this second level of meaning, often called "symbolic meaning", which must be more adequately understood if one is to comprehend the meaning of complex discourses.

CHAPTER 5

Symbolic Meaning

As already suggested in Chapter 4, the relationship between
a verbal sign and its referent in certain contexts may involve a chain of sign-referent relations. In the case of
literal meanings of a word, there is a relatively simple
relationship between a verbal sign and the referent. For
example, the Greek term αἷμα in John 19.34 designates a particular substance, namely, blood, but in Matthew 27.25, 'his
blood be on us', the term αἷμα obviously does not designate
a physiological substance but 'death'. In other words, the
meaning is 'we will be responsible for his death'. One may
describe this extended meaning of αἷμα as a sign pointing to
the substance 'blood' and the substance blood being a sign
of 'death'. In the meaning of 'death', there is a shift
from the semantic domain of physiological substance (into
which the literal meaning of αἷμα fits) to the domain of
physiological events, to which this figurative meaning of
αἷμα belongs. In the phrase 'faith in his blood' in Romans
3.25 there is still a further shift in meaning, for this is
not simply a matter of physiological death but a particular
kind of death which must be related to the sacrificial
system of atonement. In other words, this meaning of αἷμα
can only be understood in terms of a domain of religiously
relevant metaphysical events.

A similar chain of referential series exists in the case of
the term σταυρός 'cross'. In Mark 15.32 σταυρός designates
a particular instrument of execution on which Christ died,
but in the phrase 'preaching of the cross' in 1 Corinthians
1.18, the instrument of execution has become itself a sign
of Christ's death as a means of atonement. Interposed,
therefore, between the verbal sign σταυρός and the message
concerning atonement is the significance of the object sign,
namely, a particular historical cross on which Christ died.

When people speak today of "the conflict between the cross and the crescent", a still further symbolic relationship is involved, since in such a context the term <u>cross</u> refers to an institution, namely, Christendom, which has become symbolized by a particular object replicated in many different forms but dependent upon the original form of the cross on which Christ died.

In order to understand more satisfactorily the implication of such a series of sign-referent relations, it is important to consider in greater detail the basic semiotic relationships described briefly in Chapter 1. The triple relationship between the sign, referent, and the semiotic structure which makes possible that relationship is fundamental to the understanding of any and all kinds of meaning. All codes consist essentially of signs and arrangements. The arrangements may be regarded as the syntagmatic relationships, that is to say, the combinatory structures, and the system of signs which enter into such combinatory arrangements constitutes essentially the paradigmatic relationships.

Signs may, however, be viewed from a number of different perspectives. For example, (1) channels of communication, (2) types of signs, based on the relations to referents, (3) discursive and presentational signs, (4) multiple meanings of signs.

Channels of Communication

Any sensory channel may serve as a means of communication. One of the most important channels, but one which is rarely realized, is the chemical channel of communication. This is particularly important in the case of the DNA constituting the double helix in the genetic structure of all living cells. Communication by hormones also employs the chemical channel, and for insects the chemical channel of pheromones is crucial.

The channel of hearing is widely employed in the animate world. Barking of dogs, singing of birds, bugle calls, and words are all primarily communicated by hearing, but sight also is an important means of communication. Gestures, degrees of proximity, emblems, pictures, and writing are all dependent upon a channel of communication involving sight.

Touch is also an important channel of communication. A pat on the back, a handshake, intimacy in lovemaking, and for fish, apparently delicate differences in pressure communicate a great deal.

The sense of smell may also constitute a channel of communication, for there are those who insist that there is a "language of perfumes", and others are equally sure that taste is an important channel of communication, for there is presumably a "language of winetasting".

Recent experiments with birds would suggest that electromagnetic waves are somehow employed as channels of communication.

Whether signs are purposeful or not has very important implications for the interpretation of signs. The barking of a dog seems obviously purposeful, and street signs are certainly so (failure to observe them brings sanctions). The use of language is purposeful, even though we sometimes cannot determine why people say what they do. Wet streets as the result of rain do not, however, constitute purposeful signs, nor are dark clouds as a sign of rain regarded by people in the Western world as being particularly purposeful, but in some cultures of the world heavy storm clouds represent the purposeful communication of spirit beings, and even among many Christians earthquakes and droughts are regarded as purposeful signs of God's displeasure.

The degree of dependency of a particular code may be an

important factor in understanding meaning. Speech, for example, is generally regarded as relatively independent, though it may be rather heavily conditioned by external or internal conditions or circumstances. However, writing is obviously dependent upon speech, and semaphore signaling or telegraphy is in turn dependent upon a writing system.

In the case of speech there are always a number of paralinguistic features which constitute a complex set of dependent codes. Intonation, speed of utterance, tone of voice, and enunciation all serve as signs pointing to highly significant referents. The enunciation of words becomes almost a sure sign of one's geographical origin. Differences in enunciation or pronunciation may also signal such differences of status as age, sex, level of education, and communicative role (for example, preacher and parishioner). A physiological condition may also be signaled by pronunciation, particularly in cases of drunkenness or the results of a stroke.

The extralinguistic codes of body language involving gestures, stance, and muscle tension may be either independent of language or, as in many instances, closely co-ordinated with verbal and paralinguistic features.

For language one of the important problems involves the type of accompanying codes, particularly music and acting.

Types of Signs

One of the most relevant ways to understand the roles of signs is to study the way in which they relate to referents. Charles Peirce's pioneering work (1934) in distinguishing between icons, indices, and cultural conventions (which he called symbols), is in many respects fundamental to any adequate understanding of signs and referents.

As the name suggests, icons are based on a similarity of

form or function between the sign and the referent. A picture constitutes the most obvious artifactual sign, since it is a graphic portrayal of the object to which it refers. Footprints as natural signs are also icons. As Jakobson has pointed out, imitative magic fits into this same category of icons, since it becomes a behavioral sign based on similarity of activity.

Graphic forms such as diagrams, models, and graphs are also iconic signs, and the DNA which constitutes a kind of template for the RNA is likewise iconic.

Many gestures for eating and drinking are iconic in the sense that they are readily interpreted by virtue of the very clear way in which they imitate the actual processes of eating and drinking.

In terms of language, onomatopoeic expressions are purposefully iconic since they attempt by means of verbal sounds to imitate nonverbal sounds. Metaphors, since they are based upon similarity of form, function, or attributes, are likewise iconic, even as parables and allegories are typical discourse icons, and insofar as novels and short stories are symbolic representations of reality, they likewise are iconic.

Indices differ from icons in that they are based primarily upon matters of association rather than upon degrees of similarity. Wet streets as a sign of rain constitute an index because wet streets are associated with the fact of rain having recently occurred. Such artifacts as arrows or needles pointing in certain directions or to certain gradations of meters are likewise indices, and gestures of pointing belong to this same class.

A number of verbal signs are essentially indices. For example, names, pronouns, deictics (e.g. this, that, here, there), and even such a generic verbal substitute as what-chamacallit, are indices by virtue of their association with referents.

Contagious magic, since it is based upon the use of some object (fingernail, hair, bit of uneaten food, or piece of cloth associated with some person), is also essentially an indexical sign, even as are verbal metonymies, for example, the use of name in an expression such as believe in his name, when really name only stands for the person.

For this study of style and discourse it is particularly important to note that a high percentage of the rhetorical devices described in Chapter 2 function essentially as indexical signs. They acquire their semiotic significance by virtue of the fact that they are associated with certain modes and functions of communication. For many persons it may be strange to speak of rhetorical devices as having "meaning", since so often the term meaning is restricted to the lexical meaning of words involving objects, events, states, abstracts, and relations. But if we consider meaning in the larger framework of sign systems in relationship to sets of referents, one can readily understand how meaning is applicable to indices in a way closely analogous to its significance in the case of traditional lexical usage.

The third type of sign-referent relation involves those signs which are cultural conventions. These signs are essentially arbitrary. For example, in the case of words such as English boy, French garcon, German Junge, and Spanish muchacho, there is no iconic or indexical relationship between the forms of the words and the referent of these terms, namely, 'boy'. The relationship between the sounds and their referent is arbitrary, but this does not mean that the structured relationships between terms within a particular semantic domain including these words would be arbitrary, or irrational.

In addition to the numerous cultural conventions of verbal
signs, there are also similar conventions in magic, for
example, luck in carrying a rabbit's foot or good fortune to
be gained by catching a falling leaf. A number of signs employed in sign language are also arbitrary in form, and much
of abstract art may be regarded as consisting of cultural
conventions.

Discursive and Presentational Signs

The relationship of signs to discursive or presentational
modes of communication is extremely important for an
adequate comprehension of the communicative process. An
utterance consisting of words is essentially discursive, and
a set of mathematical symbols may be translated into the
discursive mode. The same is generally true of sign
language. One cannot, however, translate a graphic masterpiece into discourse. Picasso's Guernica has a symbolic
significance which can never be captured in words. The
practice of glossolalia certainly constitutes a sign, but it
does not consist of words nor is it translatable into words.
Even though there are so-called interpretations of glossolalia utterances, all analyses of such communications have
indicated clearly that there is no formal relationship between the speaking in tongues and the subsequent interpretation.

In the same way that a picture cannot really be translated
into words nor a symphony be restructured as a dialogue, so
neither can a symbolic event be turned into a discursive
substitute. Rituals such as Holy Communion and a religious
event such as the crucifixion have elements which can be
mentioned by means of words but which cannot be really
translated into words. The same is true of the artistic
features of literary productions. Though such masterpieces
consist of words, their full significance cannot be repro-
duced in discursive fashion. There are esthetic elements
which are inevitably lost in any attempt to transpose a

literary work into some descriptive substitute.

Multiple Meanings of Signs

What makes some signs particularly important is their multiple relations to referents. As Charles Peirce pointed
out, the footprints discovered by Robinson Crusoe on the
sand of his lonely island were simultaneously an icon of a
foot, an index of a person, and the symbolic evidence of a
human being having been there. Similarly, wine used in Holy
Communion is an icon of blood, an index of death, and a
symbol of identification with Christ. Even the ritual of
Holy Communion itself becomes an icon of fellowship and a
covenant relationship (in Jewish society covenants were es-
tablished by eating together), an index of remembering the
life and ministry of Christ, and a symbol of religious commitment.

One must not imagine, however, in moving from one culture to
another that the same objects will constitute signs of corresponding referents. For many Muslims, for example, the
sign of a cross has as a referent a sword (something origi-
nating at the time of the Crusades), and for many Africans
the idea of circumcising a baby at eight days of age seems
either unutterably cruel or strangely anomalous, since circumcision is usually practiced in Africa only at the age of
puberty as a mark of sexual maturity.

When Roman Catholic missionaries first entered the Tzeltal
area of southern Mexico, they were undoubtedly surprised at
the rapidity with which the people accepted the symbol of
the cross. Such a symbol, however, already existed in Tzeltal culture, but it did not refer to the death of Christ but
was a sign referring to fertility and sexual relations.

The extent to which the symbolic significance of signs may
change drastically is something experienced by practically
all religions. In North America, for example, Santa Claus

has largely replaced the creche as a sign of Advent, and the ordinance of marriage has been largely secularized.

There appears to be no end to the number of objects, events, or abstracts which may serve as signs of culturally relevant referents. In Mark 7.27-28 Jesus employs κυνάρια 'dogs' in referring to Gentiles (a popular usage in his day), but the Syrophoenician woman quickly turns this usage to her advantage by indicating that the dogs at least had the advantage of eating the crumbs which fell from the table where the children were eating. In Lk 15.8 the ten coins no doubt had special symbolic significance because they were probably a part of a bride's wedding headdress. In the Scriptures sheep and goats are often symbolic of classes of persons. In some instances the significance of a symbol is even explained in Scripture itself as in the case of incense symbolizing the prayers of the saints (Revelation 8.3), and the dragon of Revelation 12 and 13 is clearly described in terms of imperial arrogance and power.

In the Scriptures many events are regarded as particularly important symbols, for example, circumcision, sacrifice, and baptism. The resurrection of Christ becomes not only a symbol of having overcome death but a validating symbol for all those who would be his followers.

Many symbols in the New Testament are to be understood in terms of their sociological setting, for example, the fact that Jesus sat down to teach (the position of a rabbi), and the casting of garments and branches in front of Jesus as he rode into Jerusalem as a symbol of homage. In the book of John each of the miracles of Jesus is treated as a sign of his nature and power, whether it was making water into wine, restoring sight to a blind man, or feeding the five thousand.

In the Scriptures even abstracts figure importantly as symbols. Numbers such as three, seven, twelve, twenty-four, forty, and ten thousand all must be understood in certain contexts as having symbolic significance. The number forty must often be interpreted as a relatively large number for such an event, and ten thousand usually means simply an enormously large number. The various colors of the horses in Revelation 6.1-8 are certainly significant. Even the directions 'up' and 'down' and the locations 'above' and 'below' have important symbolic significance. The abstracts of 'light' and 'darkness' are particularly important symbols in the Gospel of John.

CHAPTER 6

The Meaning of Nuclear Structures

Nuclear structures constitute the core units of propositions. In a sense, they may be described as the central portion around which a sentence develops. In terms of rhetorical structures, they are not too important except in their nominalized forms, but they do figure strategically in the analysis of the meaning of internuclear structures as treated in Chapter 7.

Nuclear structures are of two principal types: participational and qualificational. Participational nuclear structures consist of a nucleus which is an event or state and a number of participants, which may be regarded as satellites. The participants in events have a number of semantic roles, for example, causative agent, immediate agent, affected participant (also often spoken of as "experiencer", if an animate being is involved), the benefactee, instrument, and content. The various ways in which participants may serve as satellites of an event nucleus can perhaps be best illustrated by a series of English sentences in which the various participants maintain the same semantic relationship to the nucleus, though they may occur in different positions.

1. John filled the tank.
    (immediate agent, nucleus, affected)
2. The tank was filled by John.
    (affected, nucleus, immediate agent)
3. Paul had John fill the tank.
    (causative agent, immediate agent, nucleus, affected)
4. The tank filled.
    (affected, nucleus)
5. The tank filled with water.
    (affected, nucleus, content)

6. The tank was filled with a hose.
(affected, nucleus, instrument)
7. Water filled the tank.
(content, nucleus, affected)
8. John filled the tank for Mary.
(immediate agent, nucleus, affected, benefactee)

To such a nuclear structure it is always possible to add
elements of time and space, for example, John filled the
tank yesterday and the tank behind the house filled quickly.
It is also possible to nominalize the nucleus and consequ-
ently to speak of the filling of the tank and John's filling
of the tank.

Nominalization, however, can involve serious ambiguities,
since in nominalization one does not usually mark clearly
the relationship between the nucleus and the satellites. For
example, the sentence exploding tanks can be dangerous can
mean that 'the task of causing tanks to explode can be dangerous' or 'the fact that tanks may explode can be dangerous'.

In the New Testament there are a number of problems resulting from nominalization of nuclear structures. Within the
broader context the relationship between the satellites and
the nucleus may be made evident, but in a number of contexts
ambiguity remains. For example, in a number of passages
expressions such as ἀγάπη θεοῦ 'love of God' may be either
'God's love for people' or 'people's love for God'.

In a number of instances nominalized phrases also exhibit
alternative orders while preserving the same meaningful
relationship between the nucleus and the satellites. Compare, for example, the promise of the Spirit (Galatians
3.14) and the Spirit of promise (Ephesians 1.13). There is,
however, a difference in meaning in these two phrases, since
in the first instance the focus is upon the promise and in

the second instance upon the Spirit. Such a distinction does have relevance for rhetorical patterns. The same type of relationship occurs in the phrases the God of peace (Romans 15.33) and the peace of God (Ephesians 1.2). In each instance it is God who is the causative agent of peace, but there certainly is a distinction in focus, and one might also describe this difference as a distinction in topic and comment. For example, in the phrase the God of peace God is the topic and the fact that he is the one who causes peace is the comment. The revers , of course, is true in the phrase the peace of God.

The degree to which a particular text employs a high percentage of nominalized expressions is a highly significant feature of discourse. In Romans 1.1-7 there are, for example, sixteen such nominalizations. Expository discourse tends to use far more nominalization than narrative discourse employs, and the degree of generalization is almost directly proportionate to the extent of nominalization. Among different writers the extent of nominalization of events (with the accompanying omission of participants) is probably one of the most characteristic hallmarks of a particular author.

In trying to determine the meaning of combinatory structures, it is entirely too easy to equate formally similar constructions and to regard them as somehow having much the same meaning. For example, in English there is a tendency to regard the following series as meaning "possession": his sins, his ruin, his punishment, his sickness, his goodness, his house, his country, his son, his arm. Though the constructions appear to be somewhat similar, the relationship between his and the following nouns is quite distinct in each case. In his sins, for example, he is the one who sins, while in his ruin, one would normally understand the phrase as meaning that he was ruined. In the case of his punishment there is an evident ambiguity, for this phrase may mean that someone receives punishment or that he is the agent of punishing others.

In many instances nominal phrases omit a statement of an underlying event or relationship, as in the series Jesus of Nazareth, the scribes of the Pharisees, and the God of Israel. In the first instance, it is 'Jesus who comes from Nazareth'; in the second case, these are 'scribes who belong to the sect of the Pharisees'; and in the third case, it is 'the God whom Israel worships' or 'the God who protects Israel'.

Qualificational nuclear structures are of four major types: (1) those which relate a non-inherent state or condition to an object, (2) those that specify some inherent attribute, (3) those which mark a member of a class, and (4) those which are equational.

Qualificational nuclear structures which indicate a state or condition imply some type of event or process. In the expression the building is ruined the indication of state, namely, ruined, implies that something has happened to cause such a state. This is somewhat different in meaning, however, from a regular passive such as the building was ruined by the bomb.

In the case of an inherent attribute, the predicate element indicates a quality, quantity, or other feature, which is in no way related to some event or process. Typical phrases would be John is tall and he is intelligent.

In qualifying an object as a member of a class, one is simply stating that what is characteristic of such a class is characteristic of that person. This applies also to instances in which there is only one unique member of such a class. In the expression John is a teacher, one must say that anything which is typical of a teacher would be typical of John, but, of course, not the reverse, for not what is typical of an individual named John would be typical of all teachers. In the case of the statement in John 1.1, the Word was God, God is a unique member of the class, but such a statement does not warrant a reversal of relationships as one early heresy did by claiming that the meaning was 'God was the Word'.

An equational relationship is typical of the statement John is the leader, in which case the subject and predicate components may be reversed so that one can also say that the leader is John.

Confusion between the meaning of qualificational nuclear structures identifying a member of a class and equational relationships is to be found in serious misinterpretations not only of the expression the Word was God but also for those who insist that God is love also means that 'love is God'. Others would reverse the statement God is spirit, and on the basis of a wrong understanding of semantic relationships in syntactic constructions they insist that this means also that 'spirit is God'.

From the standpoint of the purely formal level of language it is relevant to note the ways in which different syntactic classes function in diverse nuclear structures, but in terms of the rhetorical level of language, it is more important to consider the roles of the basic semantic classes in the diverse nuclear structures. The semantic class of objects (or entities) are primarily the participants in events, and the semantic class of events constitute the nuclear elements, while states related to events and processes constitute the qualificational elements. In qualificational nuclear structures employing the verb to be, one can best analyze the role of the verb as being essentially a marker of a relationship, but it also serves the purpose of carrying a temporal element, namely, the tense. Other verbs which likewise mark such a relationship (for example, be-

come, seem, appear) add features of process and mode as well
as temporal elements, but their principal role is to mark a
relationship.

The semantic class of abstracts primarily serve to qualify
objects, events, states, and in some instances, other abstracts.

As the name implies, relationals serve simply to relate
various semantic classes. Such relationals may be words
(e.g. for, but, because), phrases (e.g. so that, in order
to), or bound morphemes (e.g. case endings in Greek). These
relationals are often regarded as so-called "function
elements", since they function primarily to relate the principal semantic carriers of meaning, but it would be quite
wrong to regard them as being semantically empty. They do
serve as signs, and even in the case of to as a marker of
the infinitive, one may say that such a form has an indexical meaning in that it marks the presence of a postposed infinitive.

CHAPTER 7

The Meaning of Internuclear Structures

In the study of the meaning of internuclear structures (that is, structures consisting of more than one nuclear structure), it is important to focus upon three different aspects: (1) the difference between surface-level syntactic structures and the underlying meaning of both smaller and larger units, (2) the range of possible meaningful relations between different structures, and (3) the differences between syntactic and rhetorical structures.

Syntactic Structures and Underlying Meaning

The differences between surface level syntactic structures and the underlying meaning is well illustrated by two phrases in Romans 1.5: χάριν καὶ ἀποστολήν literally, 'grace and apostleship' and ὑπακοὴν πίστεως literally, 'obedience of faith'. In the first instance the conjunction καὶ and the parallel case endings would suggest a coordinate semantic relationship, but though this is true on the surface level of the syntax, it is not true of the underlying meaning, for ἀποστολήν 'apostleship' designates what is the χάριν. In other words, the phrase χάριν καὶ ἀποστολήν is perhaps best rendered as 'privilege of being an apostle', so that in reality, ἀποστολήν qualifies χάριν. Hence, rather than being semantically coordinate, the relationship is semantically subordinate. In the case of ὑπακοὴν πίστεως, however, though the syntactic structure suggests a subordinate relation, in reality these two nominalized events are a syntactic transform of a finite verb expression 'believe and obey'.

In this same verse, Romans 1.5, ἐλάβομεν is active in form but in reality is a semantic pseudopassive, for 'to receive the privilege of being an apostle' is semantically equivalent to 'being given the privilege of being an apostle'.

In Ephesians 3.12 the syntactically coordinate expression παρρησίαν καὶ προσαγωγήν is likewise semantically subordinate, for προσαγωγήν 'entrance' specifies the area of relevance for the παρρησίαν 'boldness'. The meaningful relationship may be rendered as 'boldness to enter', but in Ephesians 1.11 a syntactically subordinate construction, τὴν βουλὴν τοῦ θελήματος, is not talking about 'the will of desire' or 'the plan of purpose', but either 'will and desire' or 'plan and purpose'.

Though in so many instances a finite verb or a nonfinite verb form, or a nominalized verb constitutes the nucleus of a nuclear structure, one must not assume that this is always the case. A number of such forms may, for example, express aspect. In Acts 20.7, for example, the verb παρέτεινεν really serves as an aspect of the semantically principal element τὸν λόγον, so that the phrase as a whole, παρέτεινέν τε τὸν λόγον, means 'he continued to speak'. Similarly, in Revelation 4.8 the nominalized verb ἀνάπαυσιν combines with the verb ἔχουσιν to form an aspect of the participle λέγοντες, so that the clause καὶ ἀνάπαυσιν οὐκ ἔχουσιν ἡμέρας καὶ νυκτὸς λέγοντες means 'and they did not cease speaking day and night'. 'To cease' is not an event in and of itself but merely an aspect of some other event.

In other instances verbs or nominalized verbs may actually serve to mark voice, that is to say, to indicate the relationship between a participant and an event or state. In the expression πειρασμοῖς περιπέσητε ποικίλοις literally, 'you fall into many kinds of trials' (James 1.2) the focal semantic component is πειρασμοῖς, while περιπέσητε serves to indicate that the subject is beginning to experience certain trials. In James 1.3 there is a similar relationship between κατεργάζεται and ὑπομονήν, in which the verb κατεργάζεται simply serves as a marker of causative relationship, so that the phrase may be rendered 'causes endurance'.

Mode may also be expressed by verbs, as, for example, in Luke 13.33 in which ἐνδέχεται indicates mere possibility, while the focal semantic component of the clause is ἀπολέσθαι 'to die'. In 1 Corinthians 5.10, ὠφείλετε also indicates mode. Though it is the finite verb of the clause in which it occurs, it is really only a modal modifier of the infinitive ἐξελθεῖν 'to go out'.

Not only are there significant differences in the meaning between surface syntactic forms and underlying semantic relations, but similar distinctions also occur in larger sections. For example, in Matthew 5.13-16 there is a complete syntactic break between verse 13, which speaks of the salt of the earth, and verse 14, which introduces the theme of 'the light of the world'. There is no marked syntactic relationship between these two units, but there certainly is an important semantic relationship marked by the evident rhetorical structures. The clauses at the beginning of each unit are completely parallel, the subject of each clause is the same and in a rhetorically emphatic position, and the two key metaphors are parallel.

Meaningful Relations between Structures

Before attempting to analyze the structures of larger discourse units, it is essential to determine the range of possible meanings which exist between nuclear structures, whether on the level of individual nuclear structures or on the level of various groupings of such structures. The following outline of these different semantic relations may not ultimately prove to be completely exhaustive, but in extensive analyses of discourse structures in a number of languages, the types listed here seem to be adequate to explain all the contrasts which have been found, though undoubtedly some subtypes could be postulated. To illustrate the differences and similarities of such semantic relations, it has seemed best to employ typical English sentences.

I   Coordinate

    A   Additive

        1   Equivalent: John is stupid; he is dumb.

        2   Different

            a   Consequential: John stopped reading and looked up.

                Dick approached the lions and one of them charged (an "unfolding" structure).

            b   Nonconsequential: John was reading and Mary was sewing.

    B   Dyadic

        1   Alternative: John will do it or die in the attempt.

        2   Contrastive: He came but did not stay.

        3   Comparative: She is more intelligent than Jane.

            He did as fine a job as Bill did.

II   Subordinate

    A   Qualificational

        1   Substance

            a   Content: He said he would go. He yelled, "Stop!"

            b   Generic-Specific: John travels a lot; each year he goes to the Orient; he's in Europe each summer; and is now in South America.

        2   Character

            a   Characterization: Working for John is terrible.

            b   Manner: He came to town riding on a horse.

            c   Setting:

                1' Time: When he came, we left.

                2' Place: Being in the house, he noticed a strange noise.

                3' Circumstance: As Jim turned, Alice disappeared.

B   Logical

1   Cause-Effect: <u>John's leaving made Mary des-</u>
     <u>pondent</u>.

2   Reason-Result: <u>Because John left, he did not</u>
     <u>see Mary</u>.

3   Means-Result: <u>By coming, John saw Mary</u>.

4   Means-Purpose: <u>John came in order to see</u>
     <u>Mary</u>.

5   Condition-Result: <u>If John comes, he will see</u>
     <u>Mary</u>.

6   Basis-Inference: <u>Since John came, he must</u>
     <u>have seen Mary</u>.

7   Concession-Result: <u>Though John came, he did</u>
     <u>not see Mary</u>.

Several features of this outline require some further explanation. In the additive-equivalent relation, the two
nuclear structures are essentially saying the same thing.
This does not mean that they are completely synonymous, for
there may be significant differences in connotation. Such
relations are, however, rhetorically highly significant
since they mark emphasis.

In the additive-different relations, the consequential ones
may suggest some kind of cause-effect relations or reason-
result relations, but such a meaning is not explicitly marked. Even in those relations which are apparently nonconsequential, one might read into the statement some consequential relationship, but this could only be done on the basis
of a broader context. A context, for example, might indicate that Mary began to sew simply because John insisted on
reading and thus was not interested in paying any attention
to her. In those instances in which consequential or nonconsequential relations are overtly marked, either within
the structure or by the immediate context, then clearly such
internuclear relations should be specified under one or more
of the logical relations.

In the generic-specific semantic relation, one unit states the matter in a general sense and another unit or units contain specific examples of the more generic unit. Of course, the specific elements may precede the generic or may precede and follow.

In the illustrative example of characterization, there are two nuclear structures, though this may not appear evident at first. Working for John is equivalent to 'someone works for John'. Such a nuclear structure then serves as the subject of is terrible, which may be formulated as X is terrible, in which case X is a substitute for the subject nuclear structure. The remaining relations seem to be quite evident and straight-forward.

Though in the above outline the semantic relations between nuclear structures are illustrated by single sentences, these same relations apply to all structural levels, in other words, the relationship between clauses, sentences, paragraphs, sections, and even chapters. Entire books, for example, may be organized on the basis of generic-specific relations. An introductory chapter may state a generic proposition, and all the specific instances of such a proposition may then be detailed. Similarly, one may organize a book in terms of reason-result, either providing a series of chapters leading up to a result, or stating the result and then a series of reasons which validate the result.

Differences between Syntactic and Rhetorical Structures

In order to illustrate the manner in which one may distinguish between syntactic and rhetorical structures in the case of larger units, Matthew 5.13-16 has been selected. In the following diagrammatic analysis of the relations, the left-hand margin indicates the different syntactic units related in terms of immediate constituents. Each numbered expression consists of a single nuclear structure (though in item 12 the elliptical element has been filled out but

placed in parentheses). In the right-hand margin the semantic relations are indicated on the basis of the preceding
outline. The semantic relations exist on a number of levels
higher than those specified by the syntactic structures, but
except for items 1, 2, and 3, the semantic relations are
congruent with all the syntactically marked structures.

This section (Matthew 5.13-16) is related to the preceding
by being a characterization of ὑμῶν, the last word of verse
12, and as is noted in the discussion of the rhetorical
structure, it effectively introduces the teaching about the
Law (Matthew 5.17-20). In a sense, however, Matthew 5.13-16
is distinctive in being so neatly structured; the sets of
immediate constituents on a semantic level do not overlap or
become embedded one within another, something which is true
of many expository discourses.

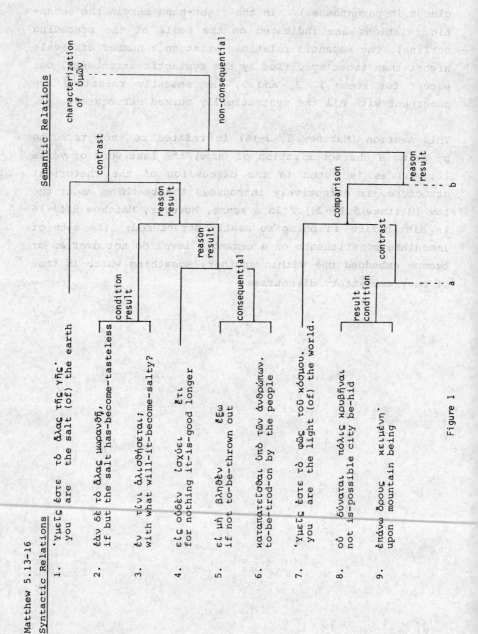

Figure 1

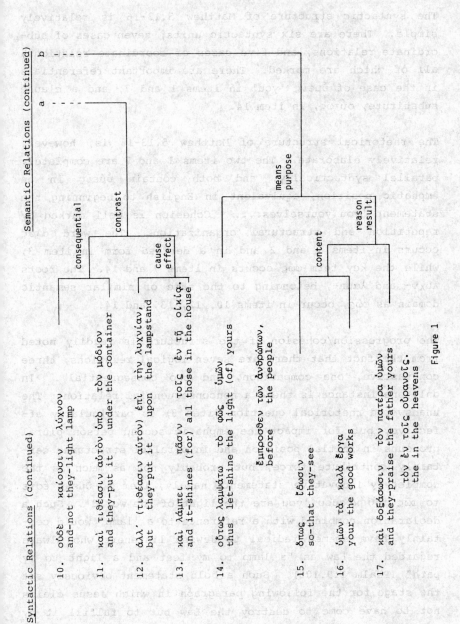

Figure 1

The syntactic structure of Matthew 5.13-16 is relatively simple. There are six syntactic units, seven cases of subordinate relations, and five cases of coordinate relations, all of which are marked. There are important referentials in the case of ὑμεῖς 'you' in items 1 and 7, and a clause substitute, οὕτως, in item 14.

The rhetorical structure of Matthew 5.13-16 is, however, relatively elaborate. The two items 1 and 7 are completely parallel syntactically, and both contain ὑμεῖς in an emphatic position, equivalent in English to beginning the statement 'you yourselves....' Cohesion is well marked by repetition and structural organization. The word ἅλας occurs in items 1 and 2 and in a derived form in item 3, while the key term φῶς occurs in items 7 and 14. The roots λυχν- and λαμπ-, belonging to the same or similar semantic domain as φῶς, occur in items 10, 12, 13, and 14.

The progression/cohesion of the structure is readily noted from the fact that there are seven logical relations, three contrastive, one comparison, and two consequential . In only one instance is there a nonconsequential relation. The unanswered rhetorical question (item 3) is particularly effective, but for impact the emphatic second person plural pronouns in initial position and in parallel structures certainly contribute force, but probably not as much as the completely innovative statement, namely, item 7, ὑμεῖς ἐστε τὸ φῶς τοῦ κόσμου 'you are the light of the world'. Such a declaration combined with a reference to a 'lamp' would certainly have seemed radical to Jewish listeners who always regarded the Law as "a lamp to my feet and a light to my path" (Psalm 119.105). Such a bold statement obviously set the stage for the following paragraph in which Jesus claims not to have come to destroy the Law but to fulfill it by giving it its true significance.

There is one possible case of hyperbole in that presumably a lamp (in item 10) on a lampstand (item 12) would give light to all those in the house (item 13). This may be either an exaggeration or a reference to a common dwelling often consisting of a single room.

Some persons have regarded item 2 as being either hyperbolic or completely contradictory, since sodium chloride cannot really become tasteless. However, as already noted, in ancient times salt was often adulterated, and in humid weather the sodium chloride would actually leech out, so that what was left was tasteless.

CHAPTER 8

Methods for the Analysis of Texts

Methods for the analysis of texts are primarily of two major types: (1) those employed in treating exposition, description, or argumentation, and (2) those employed in treating temporal sequences, for example, narrative and series of related instructions. The particular method employed in any instance depends upon the nature of the text and the purposes of the analysis.[13]

The following descriptions of methods for analyzing texts focus on rhetorical structures, so that relatively little attention will be paid to syntactic structures or to the semantics of lexical units.

Since the New Testament contains far more expository discourse than narrative (though often the expository elements are hung together by a narrative framework), it seems best to concentrate upon expository material. The first series of texts to be examined are approached by focusing upon the structural organization, whether it depends upon "stream of consciousness", as in the case of John 1.1-5 and James 1.2-8, or upon involved structural embedding, as in Hebrews 1.1-4. A more thematic approach to rhetorical structure is illustrated with Ephesians 1.3-14, which focuses upon dominant semantic factors and Romans 2.1-11, which illustrates the use of summary analysis.

The final illustrative text is the so-called Parable of the Prodigal Son (Luke 15.11-32), in which the rhetorical structure is developed in terms of a narrative scenario.

---

13   For further information with respect to methods of syntactic and semantic analysis of texts, see Eugene A. Nida, 1975, Exploring Semantic Structures, especially Chapters 3-5.

In the following diagrammatic analysis of John 1.1-5, there
are certain features which should be noted. In the left-
hand margin the syntactic relations are indicated, and
broken lines are employed to indicate the respective positions of certain key terms in juxtaposed lines. Where no
translation is necessary or warranted, an X is used, but in
general the translational equivalence is strictly literal.
One should, however, understand 'became' or 'has become' in
rendering ἐγένετο and γέγονεν, respectively, as 'came into
existence' or 'has come into existence'. In the case of
κατέλαβεν in item 10, the rendering is 'put-out' since it
refers in this context to the action of darkness upon light,
but one could render κατέλαβεν as 'overcame' or even possibly 'comprehended', since the latter is a possible meaning
even of the active form of καταλαμβάνω, though in general
'to comprehend' is a meaning of middle forms. In place of a
diagrammatic analysis of the semantic and rhetorical relationships in John 1.1-5, it seems much better to discuss
the various patterns and their relations in terms of the
sequences. Such an approach seems far more satisfactory in
the case of discourse structures which reflect relationships
best described as "stream of consciousness". In such a discourse, one simply does not find the kind of structured
hierarchy of meanings and relations found in the case of
Matthew 5.13-16.

John 1.1-5

Syntactic Relations	Semantic Relations

1. ἐν ἀρχῇ   ἦν ὁ λόγος,
   in beginning was the Word

2. καὶ ὁ λόγος ἦν πρὸς τὸν θεόν,
   and the Word was with X God

   (2 is nonconsequen-
   tial to 1, but un-
   folding and syntac-
   tically chiastic)

3. καὶ θεὸς ἦν ὁ λόγος.
   and God was the Word

   (3 is nonconsequen-
   tial and chiastic
   to 2)

4. οὗτος   ἦν ἐν ἀρχῇ
   this-one was in beginning

   πρὸς τὸν θεόν.
   with X God.

   (4 is equivalent to
   1 and 2, and parti-
   ally chiastic to 3)

5. πάντα δι'   αὐτοῦ ἐγένετο,
   all   through him   became

   (5 is characteriza-
   tion of οὗτος in 4
   in terms of role)

6. καὶ χωρὶς αὐτοῦ ἐγένετο οὐδὲ ἕν.
   and without him   became not one

   (6 is a negative
   equivalent of 5)

7. ὃ   γέγονεν   ἐν αὐτῷ ζωὴ ἦν,
   what has-become in him life was

   (7 is an unfolding
   equivalent of 5)

8. καὶ ἡ   ζωὴ ἦν τὸ φῶς
   and the life was the light (of)

   τῶν ἀνθρώπων·
   the people

   (8 is an unfolding
   consequent of 7)

9. καὶ τὸ φῶς ἐν τῇ σκοτίᾳ
   and the light in the darkness

   φαίνει,
   shines

   (9 is an unfolding
   of 8)

10. καὶ ἡ σκοτία αὐτὸ οὐ
    and the darkness it   not

    κατέλαβεν.
    put-out

    (10 is an unfolding
    of 9)

Figure 2

The syntactic structure of John 1.1-5 is relatively simple. It consists of ten units which would be called "colons" in traditional Greek grammars, but these colons are semantically linked into five sentences. The semantic relationships between these colons are, however, complex, both in terms of meaningful relationships and formal arrangements. Item 2, for example, is essentially nonconsequential to item 1, but there is an unfolding arrangement in which ὁ λόγος 'the Word' is in the position of new information in item 1 but shifts to the position of old information in item 2. There is also a syntactically chiastic patterning in items 1 and 2, in that the order A ἐν ἀρχῇ (prepositional phrase), B ἦν (verb), C ὁ λόγος (noun phrase) becomes C ὁ λόγος B ἦν A πρὸς τὸν θεόν in item 2.

Item 3 is nonconsequential to item 2, but there is a chiastic rearrangement of the nouns. There is, however, no shift between new and old information, because in item 3 θεος 'God' is a predicate qualifier of ὁ λόγος 'the Word'. The term θεός is clearly in an emphatic position.

Item 4 is equivalent to items 1 and 2, since it simply restates what is in 1 and 2. There is, however, a partial chiastic relationship between items 4 and 3, since the substitute (οὗτος) for ὁ λόγος 'the Word' is initial in 4, and θεός is final in 4.

Item 5 consists of a characterization of οὗτος in item 4, which in turn is merely a substitute for ὁ λόγος 'the Word'. This characterization, however, is in terms of activity, not nature or essence.

Item 6 preserves a certain parallelism with item 5 in view of the order of the respective prepositional phrases and finite verb forms, but there is a transposition of the reference to what came into existence. Item 6 is, however, the negative equivalent of item 5.

Item 7 may be regarded as consequential to items 5 and 6, and it also has an unfolding relationship to item 6 in that what is new information in 6 becomes old information in 7, that is to say, it shifts from the predicate to a subject position. Semantically one may say that item 7 is at least a partial equivalent of item 5 in that it elaborates upon the implication of 5.

There is a textual problem involved in the sequence of items 6 and 7 in that ὃ γέγονεν at the beginning of 7 can be interpreted as a relative clause qualifying οὐδὲ ἕν, but such an expression would be redundant with the statement in item 6. Furthermore, because of the tendency to pick up items in the predicate of one expression and make it the subject of the next, most critical Greek texts have interpreted ὃ γέγονεν as the subject of colon 7.

Item 8 is consequential to item 7, with an unfolding relationship in that ζωή in the predicate of 7 becomes the subject of 8. Item 9 may be regarded as consequential to item 8, with a similar unfolding relationship between predicate and subject position.

Item 10 may be regarded as consequential to item 9, particularly in view of the unfolding relationship in which an item in the predicate of item 9 becomes the subject of item 10. This pattern of unfolding relationships may be regarded as a kind of tangential elaboration of a theme. This process involves picking up new elements in the predicate of successive statements and elaborating these. In the Gospel of John this pattern is not, however, restricted to series of individual colons but is also typical of paragraphs and even of larger sections. For this reason the Gospel of John is not the kind of text which can be readily "outlined". The logic is a kind of unfolding logic rather than one of cause-effect, reason-result, means-purpose, etc. In the Gospel of John one can recognize consequential relationships, but it is a tenuous logic.

Certain additional rhetorical features of this passage should be carefully noted. For example, the verb ἦν rendered simply as 'was' in English actually has three different meanings in the first three items. In item 1 the meaning of ἦν is 'existed', in item 2 ἦν means 'was in a place', and in item 3 ἦν means 'had the nature of'. In item 8 ἦν means 'to belong to the class of'.

In item 1 the first phrase ἐν ἀρχῇ 'in the beginning' is an evident allusion to the first verse of the book of Genesis. The repetition of ἐν ἀρχῇ in item 4 and the emphasis upon the creative role of the Word reinforces this interpretation of the allusion.

The extent of syntactic and lexical chiasm is certainly an important element in this discourse. The syntactic chiasm in items 1 (ABC) and 2 (CBA) and the lexical or referential chiasm in items 2 (λόγος...θεόν) and 3 (θεός...λόγος), 3 (θεός...λόγος) and 4 (οὗτος...θεόν), and 6 (χωρὶς αὐτοῦ ἐγένετο οὐδὲ ἕν) and 7 (ὃ γέγονεν ἐν αὐτῷ) cannot be merely accidental. There is a mixture of parallelism and chiasm in items 9 and 10, in that the relationship between the subject and the verb in each case is parallel, but there is a chiastic relationship between φῶς 'light' and σκοτία 'darkness', if one regards αὐτό 'it' as a structural substitute for φῶς 'light', (φῶς...σκοτία...σκοτία...αὐτό).

It is interesting to note that the verb ἦν in items 1-4 always occurs medially, but in items 5, 6, 7, 8, and 9 the verbs alternate between final and medial position. In item 10 the verb is final, in parallel position with φαίνει, with which it contrasts strikingly.

The figurative usage of λόγος 'Word', φῶς 'light', and σκοτία 'darkness' is highly significant, as is also the po-

sition of θεός in item 3. This position is not merely a
matter of chiastic structuring. By being initial to the
colon, θεός emphasizes the deity of the Word.

The rhetorical impact of this passage was no doubt heightened for those who first received it in view of certain background knowledge which they had concerning the concept of
λόγος as the wisdom and revelation of God, a particularly
important theme developed in the Wisdom Literature of the
Old Testament. The fact that the wisdom of God was reckoned
as a creative force simply reinforces the connection made
between λόγος and that which came into existence through
him. The focus upon the λόγος as an expression of the
wisdom of God is likewise reinforced by the introduction of
φῶς 'light'. Accordingly, even from a strictly thematic
analysis of this passage, one can readily see how the formal
rhetorical features heighten the impact.

In the diagrammatic structuring of James 1.2-8 the syntactic
structure is given in the left-hand margin. This includes
two instances of embedding, one contiguous (13 and 14 are
contiguous to 12), and one case of noncontiguous embedding,
the relationship of 24 and 25 to an element in 22.

There are only five complete sentences in this somewhat longer discourse, but in each case the successive clause or
sentence picks up an item near the end of the preceding sentence, and uses this as a point of departure for elaboration. The relationship between these linking devices is
marked by broken lines. In certain respects, therefore, the
structure of James 1.2-8 parallels that of John 1.1-5 in
that an element in the predicate of one sentence is picked
up as the topic for the following sentence. This means that
James 1.2-8 also illustrates a structure based on "stream of
consciousness".

James 1.2-8

Syntactic Relations

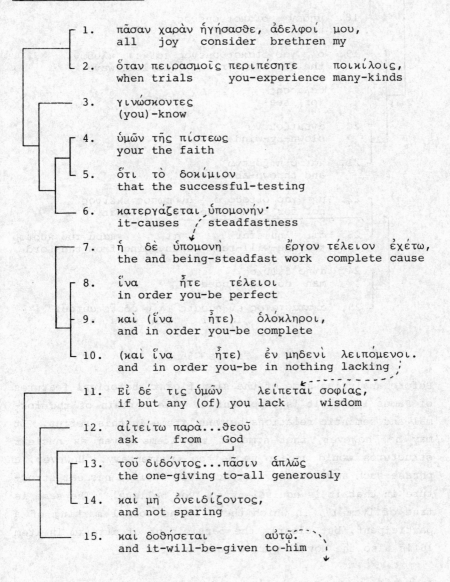

1. πᾶσαν χαρὰν ἡγήσασθε, ἀδελφοί μου,
   all joy consider brethren my

2. ὅταν πειρασμοῖς περιπέσητε ποικίλοις,
   when trials you-experience many-kinds

3. γινώσκοντες
   (you)-know

4. ὑμῶν τῆς πίστεως
   your the faith

5. ὅτι τὸ δοκίμιον
   that the successful-testing

6. κατεργάζεται ὑπομονήν·
   it-causes steadfastness

7. ἡ δὲ ὑπομονὴ ἔργον τέλειον ἐχέτω,
   the and being-steadfast work complete cause

8. ἵνα ἦτε τέλειοι
   in order you-be perfect

9. καὶ (ἵνα ἦτε) ὁλόκληροι,
   and in order you-be complete

10. (καὶ ἵνα ἦτε) ἐν μηδενὶ λειπόμενοι.
    and in order you-be in nothing lacking

11. Εἰ δέ τις ὑμῶν λείπεται σοφίας,
    if but any (of) you lack wisdom

12. αἰτείτω παρά...θεοῦ
    ask from God

13. τοῦ διδόντος...πᾶσιν ἁπλῶς
    the one-giving to-all generously

14. καὶ μὴ ὀνειδίζοντος,
    and not sparing

15. καὶ δοθήσεται αὐτῷ.
    and it-will-be-given to-him

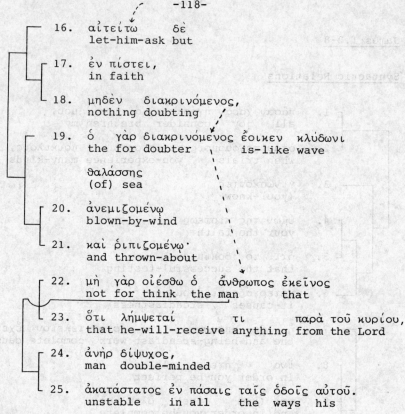

16. αἰτείτω   δὲ
    let-him-ask but

17. ἐν πίστει,
    in faith

18. μηδὲν διακρινόμενος,
    nothing doubting

19. ὁ γὰρ διακρινόμενος ἔοικεν κλύδωνι
    the for doubter   is-like wave

    θαλάσσης
    (of) sea

20. ἀνεμιζομένῳ
    blown-by-wind

21. καὶ ῥιπιζομένῳ·
    and thrown-about

22. μὴ γὰρ οἰέσθω ὁ ἄνθρωπος ἐκεῖνος
    not for think the man   that

23. ὅτι λήμψεταί   τι   παρὰ τοῦ κυρίου,
    that he-will-receive anything from the Lord

24. ἀνὴρ δίψυχος,
    man double-minded

25. ἀκατάστατος ἐν πάσαις ταῖς ὁδοῖς αὐτοῦ.
    unstable   in all   the ways his

Figure 3

Before analyzing some of the significant rhetorical features
of James 1.2-8, it is important to note certain of the formal and semantic relations between items in this series. It
may be, however, that some of the items given as nuclear
structures would appear to be too fragmentary. However, a
phrase such as ὑμῶν τῆς πίστεως (item 4) is a nuclear structure in that it is equivalent to 'you believe' The same is
true of item 17, in which there is no formal marking of a
participant, but clearly the participant of αἰτείτω in item
16 is also the covert participant in item 17.

Item 1 is probably best regarded as the result of item 2; in
other words, it is the experiencing of many kinds of trials

which should produce the joy. On the other hand, it is also possible to regard item 2 as simply the circumstantial setting for item 1 rather than the means of item 1.

Items 3-6 constitute the reason with items 1 and 2. In other words, it is the knowledge that steadfastness results from being successfully tested which is the reason for the result in item 1.

Item 4 is the affected element of item 5, that is to say, it is the faith which is subject to testing, and items 4-6 are the content of item 3. At the same time, items 4 and 5 constitute the condition or the cause of item 6. In other words, if the testing of one's faith proves its genuineness, the result is steadfastness. Item 6 is clearly the result of items 4 and 5, whether the result of a condition or of a cause.

Items 7-10 serve as a characterization of ὑπομονή in the predicate of item 6. Item 7 may be regarded as the means of items 8-10, which conversely serve as the purpose of 7. However, items 8, 9, and 10 are essentially equivalent one to the other. In the Greek text they are coordinate elements, but as indicated in figure 3, there are structural ellipses.

Items 11-15 are qualificational and contrastive to the phrase μηδενὶ λειπόμενοι in item 10 by introducing a possible exception. Item 11 serves as the condition of items 12-15. The unit 12-15 is the result of item 11, but there are important internal relations. Items 13 and 14, for example, are characterizations of θεοῦ 'God' in item 12. Item 14 is simply the negative equivalent of 13, while item 15 is the result of 12. Item 12 in a sense serves as an expression of means with item 15.

Items 16-21 serve as a contrast to items 11-15, and item 16 in itself is equivalent to 12, while items 17 and 18 constitute the condition for 16.

Item 18 is merely a negative equivalent of item 17.

Items 19-21 constitute a reason with items 17 and 18 and also a characterization of διακρινόμενος 'doubting' in 18. Items 20 and 21 are equivalent, and the two together form a characterization of κλύδωνι 'wave' in 19, which is a simile of ὁ διακρινόμενος 'one who doubts'.

Items 22-25 are a characterization of ὁ διακρινόμενος 'one who doubts' in item 19, while items 24 and 25 are a further characterization of the same person, though related in this context to ὁ ἄνθρωπος ἐκεῖνος 'that man'. Item 23 is merely the content of item 22 as that which is 'thought'. Items 24 and 25 are merely equivalent, and 25 may be regarded as essentially a negative expression corresponding to 24.

Though the structure of James 1.2-8 is considerably more complex than in the case of John 1.1-5, the basic structure reflects a stream of consciousness orientation, with repetition being one of the links, as in items 6 and 7, 10 and 11, 16 and 12, and 22 and 19. Though the text does have certain so-called conjunctive links between sentences (three occurrences of δέ and two occurrences of γάρ), these are relatively weak transitional devices.

Though the sentences in James 1.2-8 have several clauses each, the passage consists primarily of what may be called "right-hand extensions", that is to say, the sentence could be terminated at various points, but additions are made which formally tie the clauses or phrases together as a single sentence. Such sentences differ dramatically from sentences which involve "left-hand extensions", that is to say, a series of clauses and phrases which cannot be syntactically terminated before the final expression. The first type of sentence structure is often spoken of as "running style", while the second type is usually characterized as "periodic".

James 1.2-8 contains several instances of effective emphasis by means of the position of words. The phrase πᾶσαν χαράν at the beginning of item 1 is certainly in an unusual position and thus calls special attention to what must have been regarded as an anomaly, namely, the fact that many kinds of trials could be the source of 'complete joy'. The adjective ποικίλοις 'many kinds' in item 2 is likewise in an emphatic position. The verb αἰτείτω beginning item 16 is likewise emphatic.

The introduction of ἀδελφοί μου in item 1 serves a significant phatic function in identifying the writer with his readers.

One of the significant rhetorical elements in this passage is the use of figurative language, for example, περιπέσητε (item 2), the personification of ὑπομονή in item 7 as an active agent, the elaborate simile concerning κλύδωνι in items 19, 20, and 21, and the metaphors in items 24 and 25.

The passage also makes use of important contrasts, for example, between trials and joy, between not lacking and lacking, between generosity and sparing, between faith and doubting. A number of semantic parallels are also employed to reinforce meaning, for example, ἡγήσασθε 'consider' (item 1) and γινώσκοντες 'know' (item 3), κατεργάζεται 'cause' (item 6) and ἐχέτω 'cause' (item 7), τέλειοι 'perfect' (item 8) and ὁλόκληροι 'complete' (item 9), ἀνεμιζομένῳ 'blown by the wind' (item 20) and ῥιπιζομένῳ 'thrown about' (item 21), and δίψυχος 'double-minded' (item 24) and ἀκατάστατος 'unstable' (item 25).

The overall thematic content and structure of James 1.2-8 suggests a typical homily, and the rest of the book of James may be similarly characterized as a series of sermonic advice on a loosely linked series of topics.

Hebrews 1.1-4 is much more complexly organized than most brief discourse units in the New Testament. As noted in figure 4, it consists essentially of two major syntactic units, though it is also possible to construe units 5-11 as being simply a continuation of units 1-4, in that the introductory relative may be regarded as a dependent reference to υἱῷ in item 2. On the other hand, an initial ὅς which is not syntactically parallel with preceding relative clauses may be regarded as introducing a completely new colon and in this case a new sentence.

Hebrews 1.1-4

Syntactic structure

1. πολυμερῶς καὶ πολυτρόπως πάλαι ὁ
   in-many-parts and in-many-ways in-the-past X

   θεὸς λαλήσας τοῖς πατράσιν ἐν τοῖς
   God having-spoken (to) the ancestors by the

   προφήταις
   prophets

2. ἐπ᾽ ἐσχάτου τῶν ἡμερῶν τούτων
   at last (of) the days these

   ἐλάλησεν ἡμῖν ἐν υἱῷ,
   spoke to-us by son

3. ὃν ἔθηκεν κληρονόμον πάντων,
   whom he-made heir (of) all

4. δι᾽ οὗ καὶ ἐποίησεν τοὺς αἰῶνας·
   through whom also he-created the ages

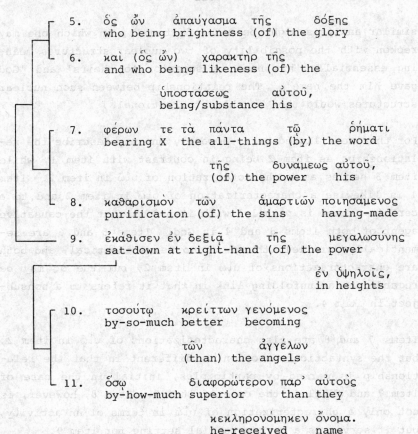

5. ὃς ὢν ἀπαύγασμα τῆς δόξης
who being brightness (of) the glory

6. καὶ (ὃς ὢν) χαρακτὴρ τῆς
and who being likeness (of) the

ὑποστάσεως αὐτοῦ,
being/substance his

7. φέρων τε τὰ πάντα τῷ ῥήματι
bearing X the all-things (by) the word

τῆς δυνάμεως αὐτοῦ,
(of) the power his

8. καθαρισμὸν τῶν ἁμαρτιῶν ποιησάμενος
purification (of) the sins having-made

9. ἐκάθισεν ἐν δεξιᾷ τῆς μεγαλωσύνης
sat-down at right-hand (of) the power

ἐν ὑψηλοῖς,
in heights

10. τοσούτῳ κρείττων γενόμενος
by-so-much better becoming

τῶν ἀγγέλων
(than) the angels

11. ὅσῳ διαφορώτερον παρ᾽ αὐτοὺς
by-how-much superior than they

κεκληρονόμηκεν ὄνομα.
he-received name

Figure 4

As may be readily noted from a careful reading of Hebrews
1.1-4, the semantic relationships between nuclear structures
are far more complex than the syntactic relations would seem
to imply. In fact, a number of linguists would no doubt
wish to break up some of the kernel-like units into a
greater number of nuclear structures. For example,
πολυμερῶς καὶ πολυτρόπως might very well be considered as
either two different circumstantial settings or as a more or
less synonymous reference to a single circumstantial setting. Others might wish to separate τῆς δυνάμεως αὐτοῦ 'of
his power' in item 7 as likewise a separate nuclear structure which would be a characterization of ῥήματι 'word'. A

similar analysis might be made of item 11, in which one may reckon with the possibility of two nuclear structures meaning essentially 'his name is superior to theirs' and 'God gave him the name'. The relationship between such nuclear structures would then be characterizational.

For the items listed here, however, one may describe the relationships as item 2 being in contrast with item 1, while item 3 serves as a characterization of υἱῷ in item 2. Item 4 is likewise a characterization of υἱῷ in item 2 and to a certain extent is parallel with item 3 in that the causative agent of both items 3 and 4 is God. Items 5 and 6 are semantically parallel, though by no means identical, and both are characterizations of υἱῷ in item 2, but the ὅς may be regarded as an unfolding link in that it refers to a nonsubject in item 4.

Items 7 and 8 are also characterizations of υἱῷ in item 2, but the syntactic connection is different in that the relationship is marked by participles, initial in the case of item 7 and final in the case of item 8. Item 8, however, is not only a characterization of υἱῷ in terms of an activity, but it serves as a circumstantial setting for item 9.

Item 9 also serves as a characterization of υἱῷ, and it is consequentially related to item 8. Items 10 and 11 relate to one another as dyadic comparisons, but the two serve also as a characterization of υἱῷ in item 2, but relate specifically to the subject of item 9.

There are a number of significant rhetorical features in Hebrews 1.1-4. Repetition of the sound of π is particularly conspicuous in item 1, occurring as it does five times in word initial position. The repetition of the morpheme πολυ- in πολυμερῶς and πολυτρόπως also highlights the fact of variety of revelations in the past in contrast with the unique revelation of God by means of his son. It is uncertain whether πολυμερῶς and πολυτρόπως are to be understood as essentially synonymous or as meaning 'fragmentary and in varied ways'. Most scholars see some distinction in meaning, though it is quite evident that the two semantically reinforce one another.

In items 1 and 2 there is a significant parallelism involving the order of time, communication, and means, so that πάλαι corresponds to ἐπ᾽ ἐσχάτου τῶν ἡμερῶν τούτων, λαλήσας corresponds to ἐλάλησεν, and ἐν τοῖς προφήταις corresponds to ἐν υἱῷ.

In items 2, 3, and 4 references to 'the son' are backgrounded, but beginning in item 5 and continuing through item 10 references to the son are foregrounded, that is to say, they become subject elements. The indirect reference to God as the implied causitive agent of item 11 tends to round out the references to God in items 1-4 and thus produce what Greek rhetoricians would regard as a periodic structure. In items 3 and 4 the focus is upon what God does to and through Christ, while in items 5 and 6 there is a description of the nature of Christ in relationship to God. Items 7, 8, and 9 speak of what Christ does and items 10 and 11 refer to Christ's status in view of the name given to him by God.

The number of figurative meanings in this relatively brief introduction to the book of Hebrews is rather outstanding: κληρονόμον 'heir', ἀπαύγασμα 'brightness', δόξης 'glory' (an indirect reference to God), χαρακτήρ 'likeness', καθαρισμόν 'purification', ἐκάθισεν 'sat down', ἐν δεξιᾷ 'at the right hand', τῆς μεγαλωσύνης ἐν ὑψηλοῖς 'of the majesty on high' (a reference to God), and ὄνομα 'name' (a reference to status).

Not only is this introduction elegantly structured in terms of the internal relationships of the parts, but it forms a very effective introduction to the following section (a typical feature of Hebrews) which deals with the superiority of the son over the angels.

It is also possible to study a text from the standpoint of certain dominant themes, as reflected in the choice of key terms or expressions which may be repeated at various strategic times within a text. Any attempt, however, to develop a thematic approach to a text must be based upon some clear indication by the text itself as to the relevance of such a thematic approach. In the case of Ephesians 1.3-14, which constitutes one syntactic unit (that is to say, one sentence), there is a significant play on the meaning of εὐλογέω in verse 3 which provides a basis for understanding two of the important themes of this unique unit. In verse 3, εὐλογητός has the meaning of 'praise' (one of the important meanings of εὐλογέω), while εὐλογήσας in verse 3 means 'to bless'. This meaning is reinforced by the phrase ἐν πάσῃ εὐλογίᾳ 'by means of every blessing'. In verses 4-14 there are fifteen different blessings mentioned, making a total of seventeen references to blessing (if one counts the two terms, εὐλογήσας and εὐλογίᾳ, as being generic references to blessing in verse 3). Another significant thematic element is the occurrence of the morpheme προ six times, either as a morphologically independent or dependent element.

An important thematic contrast in Ephesians 1.3-14 is the series of references to God and to Jesus Christ. God is identified in nominal form only twice, though he is marked as the subject five times, by pronouns ten times, and as an implicit agent twice, but Jesus Christ is identified by nominal forms seven times and by pronominal forms eight times. A careful analysis of these references indicates clearly that God is the causative agent throughout this passage, while Jesus Christ is the immediate agent, the one through whom God makes possible all of the blessings which he has determined in advance. The theme of praise is repeated at strategic points in verses 3, 6, 12, and 14.

In order to obtain some visual impression of the thematic structuring of Ephesians 1.3-14, one can employ statistical charting, as in Figure 5.

EPHESIANS 1.3-14

Verse	God	Jesus Christ	Praise	Blessing	Prior Activity or Decision
3	N N	N N	P	B B	προ
4	S P	P		B	προ-
5	S P P	N		B	
6	P S	N		B	
7	P S	P P		B B B	
8	S			B	
9	P P S	P		B	προ-
10	O P	N P		B	προ- προ-
11	O P	N P		B	προ- προ-
12	O	P P	P	B B B	
13	P	P	P	B B	
14	P		P		
TOTALS	19	15	4	17	6
	nouns=2 (N)	nouns=7 (N)	P='praise'	B='blessing'	
	pronoun=10 (P)	pronouns=8 (P)			
	suffix=5 (S)				
	covert reference =2 (O)				

Figure 5

Though Ephesians 1.3-14 is syntactically quite complex, its thematic structure is relatively simple, and it seems particularly significant that all five major thematic elements in verses 3-14 are clearly introduced in the first two verses.

A structural analysis based on statistically frequent features is often useful as a rapid review of primary participants and repeated themes or motifs, particularly in view of the repetition of words or terms belonging to the same semantic domains. The plotting of the sequences also helps one to see the way in which themes are developed.

Probably the most important rhetorical device illustrated by Ephesians 1.3-14 is the intricate foregrounding and backgrounding, which is clearly done with skill and evident theological intent. By means of lexical emphasis (that is by repeating the name of Christ seven times) the role of Christ as the immediate agent is put into focus, while the role of God as the causative agent is lexically backgrounded, but pervasive.

After making an analysis of the basic syntactic units, it is sometimes useful and appropriate to move directly to an analysis of the relationship between such units rather than necessarily treating all of the underlying relationships between individual nuclear structures. In fact, it may sometimes be helpful to make an analysis of the somewhat larger units before analyzing the detailed relationships between nuclear structures. In reality, of course, in any practical analysis one tends to do both types of analysis at the same time. One cannot arrive at a fully satisfactory treatment of the detailed relationships between nuclear structures without understanding something of the higher level relationships and vice versa.

An analysis of Romans 2.1-11 may be helpful in illustrating this particular approach. The following text is broken up in terms of nuclear structures with a number of ellipses filled out (these are clearly marked by parentheses).

An outline of the immediate constituent structures occurs in the left-hand margin, and in the right-hand margin brackets indicate the major structures which are identified by letters A, B, C, D, E, F, G, H.

Because the structure is so complex, it may be helpful in getting at the meaning to follow the translation of this material in the TEV text which immediately follows the Greek diagrammatic structure.

Romans 2.1-11

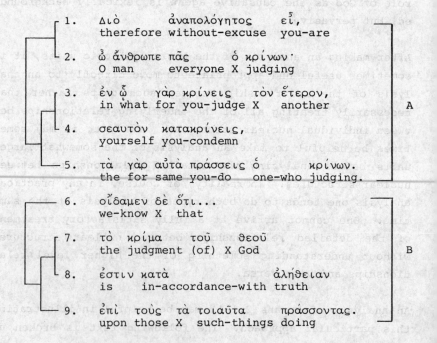

1. Διὸ   ἀναπολόγητος   εἶ,
   therefore without-excuse   you-are

2. ὦ ἄνθρωπε πᾶς   ὁ κρίνων·
   O man   everyone X judging

3. ἐν ᾧ   γὰρ κρίνεις   τὸν ἕτερον,
   in what for you-judge X   another   A

4. σεαυτὸν κατακρίνεις,
   yourself you-condemn

5. τὰ γὰρ αὐτὰ πράσσεις ὁ   κρίνων.
   the for same you-do   one-who judging.

6. οἴδαμεν δὲ ὅτι...
   we-know X that

7. τὸ κρίμα   τοῦ θεοῦ
   the judgment (of) X God   B

8. ἐστιν κατὰ   ἀλήθειαν
   is   in-accordance-with truth

9. ἐπὶ τοὺς τὰ τοιαῦτα   πράσσοντας.
   upon those X such-things doing

```
  ┌──  10.  λογίζη        δὲ τοῦτο,
  │         do-you-think X  this
  │        ─────────────────────────
╭─┤     ┌── 11.  ὦ ἄνθρωπε ὁ κρίνων
│ │     │        O man       X judging
│ │  ┌──┤
│ │  │  │── 12.  τοὺς τὰ τοιαῦτα    πράσσοντας
│ │  │  │        those X  such things doing
│ └──┤  │
│    │  └── 13.  καὶ ποιῶν αὐτά,
│    │           and doing the-same
│    │
│    │  ┌── 14.  ὅτι σὺ ἐκφεύξῃ
│    └──┤        that you will-escape
│       │
│       └── 15.  τὸ κρίμα    τοῦ  θεοῦ;
│                the judgment (of) X God
│
│       ┌── 16.  ἢ τοῦ πλούτου τῆς   χρηστότητος αὐτοῦ
│       │        or the riches (of) X kindness    his
│    ┌──┤
│    │  │── 17.  καὶ τῆς ἀνοχῆς        (αὐτοῦ)
│    │  │        and X    forebearance his
│    │  │
│    │  │── 18.  καὶ τῆς μακροθυμίας (αὐτοῦ)
│    │  │        and X    patience    his
│    │  │
│    │  └── 19.  καταφρονεῖς,
│    │           do-you-despise
├────┤
│    │  ┌── 20.  ἀγνοῶν     ὅτι...
│    │  │        not-knowing that
│    └──┤
│       │── 21.  τὸ χρηστὸν τοῦ   θεοῦ
│       │        the goodness (of) X God
│       │
│       └── 22.  εἰς μετάνοιάν σε ἄγει;
│                to  repentance you leads
│
│       ┌── 23.  κατὰ        δὲ τὴν σκληρότητά σου
│    ┌──┤        because-of X  the hardness    your
│    │  │
│    │  └── 24.  καὶ (κατὰ)      ἀμετανόητον καρδίαν
│    │           and because-of unrepentant heart
│    │
│    │── 25.  θησαυρίζεις    σεαυτῷ      ὀργὴν
│    │        you-treasure-up for-yourself anger
└────┤
     │  ┌── 26.  ἐν ἡμέρᾳ ὀργῆς
     │  │        in day  (of) anger
     │  │
     └──┤── 27.  καὶ (ἐν ἡμέρᾳ) ἀποκαλύψεως
        │        and  in day  (of) revelation
        │
        └── 28.  δικαιοκρισίας       τοῦ  θεοῦ,
                 (of) righteousness (of) X God
```

C

D

E

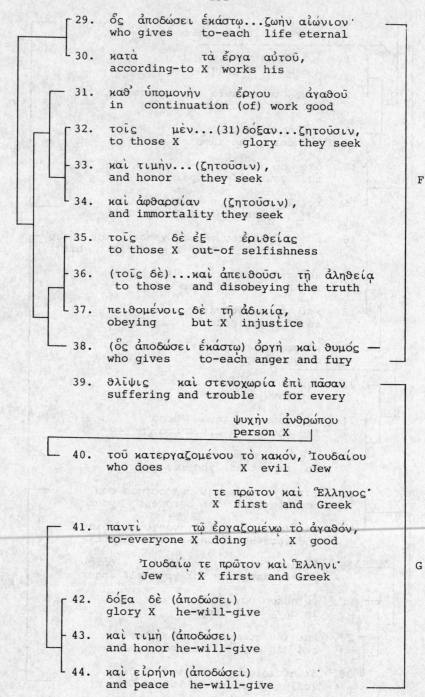

```
┌─ 29.  ὃς  ἀποδώσει  ἑκάστῳ...ζωὴν αἰώνιον·          ─┐
│       who gives      to-each  life eternal          │
└─ 30.  κατὰ         τὰ ἔργα  αὐτοῦ,                   │
        according-to X  works his                     │
   31.  καθ᾽ ὑπομονὴν    ἔργου    ἀγαθοῦ              │
        in   continuation (of) work good              │
   32.  τοῖς    μὲν...(31)δόξαν...ζητοῦσιν,            │
        to those X           glory   they seek         │
   33.  καὶ τιμὴν...(ζητοῦσιν),                        │
        and honor    they seek                    F    │
   34.  καὶ ἀφθαρσίαν  (ζητοῦσιν),                     │
        and immortality they seek                      │
   35.  τοῖς    δὲ ἐξ    ἐριθείας                      │
        to those X  out-of selfishness                 │
   36.  (τοῖς δὲ)...καὶ ἀπειθοῦσι  τῇ  ἀληθείᾳ        │
         to those  and disobeying the truth            │
   37.  πειθομένοις δὲ  τῇ ἀδικίᾳ,                     │
        obeying      but X  injustice                  │
   38.  (ὃς ἀποδώσει ἑκάστῳ) ὀργὴ  καὶ θυμός —        ─┘
        who gives    to-each anger and fury

   39.  θλῖψις    καὶ στενοχωρία ἐπὶ πᾶσαν            ─┐
        suffering and trouble      for every           │

                    ψυχὴν  ἀνθρώπου                    │
                    person X                           │

   40.  τοῦ κατεργαζομένου τὸ κακόν, Ἰουδαίου          │
        who does           X  evil   Jew               │

                    τε πρῶτον καὶ  Ἕλληνος·            │
                    X  first  and  Greek               │

   41.  παντὶ         τῷ ἐργαζομένῳ τὸ ἀγαθόν,         │
        to-everyone X  doing         X  good           │

                    Ἰουδαίῳ τε πρῶτον καὶ Ἕλληνι·  G   │
                    Jew     X  first  and Greek        │

   42.  δόξα  δὲ (ἀποδώσει)                            │
        glory X   he-will-give                         │

   43.  καὶ τιμὴ (ἀποδώσει)                            │
        and honor he-will-give                         │

   44.  καὶ εἰρήνη (ἀποδώσει)                         ─┘
        and peace   he-will-give
```

———— 45. οὐ γάρ ἐστιν προσωπολημψία παρὰ τῷ θεῷ. ⎤ H
           not for is   favoritism   with X God ⎦

Figure 6

(TEV translation of Romans 2.1-11)

"Do you, my friend, pass judgment on others? You have no excuse at all, whoever you are. For when you judge others and then do the same things which they do, you condemn yourself. [2]We know that God is right when he judges the people who do such things as these. [3]But you, my friend, do those very things for which you pass judgment on others! Do you think you will escape God's judgment? [4]Or perhaps you despise his great kindness, tolerance, and patience. Surely you know that God is kind, because he is trying to lead you to repent. [5]But you have a hard and stubborn heart, and so you are making your own punishment even greater on the Day when God's anger and righteous judgments will be revealed. [6]For God will reward every person according to what he has done. [7]Some people keep on doing good, and seek glory, honor, and immortal life; to them God will give eternal life. [8]Other people are selfish and reject what is right, in order to follow what is wrong; on them God will pour out his anger and fury. [9]There will be suffering and pain for all those who do what is evil, for the Jews first and also for the Gentiles. [10]But God will give glory, honor, and peace to all who do what is good, to the Jews first and also to the Gentiles. [11]For God judges everyone by the same standard."

In order to analyze the relationship between the major syntactic and semantic units, it is usually helpful to summarize in précis form the summary meaning of each unit. The following series of A-H represent this kind of summarization.

A   You have no excuse for condemning another while being guilty of doing the same.

B   God's judgment against such a person is right.

C   God's judgment cannot be escaped.

D   You are despising God's present kindness, meant to lead to repentance.

E   Your attitude will bring even greater condemnation.

F   God will judge all according to what they have done.

G   God makes no difference between Jews and non-Jews.

H   God does not show favoritism.

One may then state the relationship between these units in the following manner:

A is consequential to the immediately preceding statement in Romans 1.32.

B is a characterization of the judgment implied in A and specified in Romans 1.32.

C is the result of A-B.

D is consequential to A-C.

E is the result of D.

F is the result of A-E.

G is specific to F as a generic.

H is the reason for G.

As will be immediately evident from the above statements of relationships between these higher level units, the relationships are not necessarily limited to immediately juxtaposed units. Matters of reason-result, means-purpose, generic-specific, or consequentials may overlap several units, so that one must deal with various patterns of immediate constituent relations on a semantic level.

This section of Romans 2.1-11 has been purposely chosen because of its structural complexity consisting of relatively

long sentences, considerable embedding, heavy ellipsis, anacolutha, and considerable parallelism and contrast. A brief
analysis of some of the principal rhetorical features indicates clearly how neatly structured this passage is:

1. The connective διό is emphatic and marks a conclusion to what has just been said at the end of Romans 1.

2. The vocative phrases ὦ ἄνθρωπε πᾶς ὁ κρίνων and ὦ
   ἄνθρωπε ὁ κρίνων (items 2 and 11) serve to emphasize the second person reference.

3. The second person singular reference serves to
   make the statement more personally applicable, and
   it may carry some of the "personalized" connotations of the second person singular used so frequently in the Hebrew Old Testament and reflected
   in admonitions in the Septuagint.

4. The frequent repetition of the root κριν- (or the
   variant κρι-) in items 2, 3, 4, 5, 7, 11, 15, and
   28 serves to emphasize the fact of judgment and to
   tie the structure together. In the latter part of
   this section, the root κριν- is dropped, but an
   even more emphatic term is employed, namely ὀργή,
   in items 25, 26, and 38.

5. The effective combination of positional chiasm and
   contrastive parallelism in κρίνεις τὸν ἕτερον,
   σεαυτὸν κατακρίνεις (items 3 and 4) is extremely
   effective.

6. A number of parallel phrases occur, as in τὰ γὰρ
   αὐτὰ πράσσεις (item 5), τοὺς τὰ τοιαῦτα πράσσοντας
   (item 9), and τοὺς τὰ τοιαῦτα πράσσοντας (item
   12). Compare also τὸ κρίμα τοῦ θεοῦ (item 7) and
   τὸ κρίμα τοῦ θεοῦ (item 15).

7. There are also a number of sets of three lexical
   items: τῆς χρηστότητος, τῆς ἀνοχῆς, and τῆς
   μακροθυμίας (items 16-18); δόξαν, τιμήν, and
   ἀφθαρσίαν (items 32-34); τοῖς δὲ ἐξ ἐριθείας,

ἀπειθοῦσι τῇ ἀληθείᾳ, and πειθομένοις δὲ τῇ ἀδικίᾳ (items 35-37); and δόξα, τιμή, and εἰρήνη (items 42-44).

8   This passage is particularly heavy with nomina-lized events and/or states as in items 7, 15, 16, 17, 18, 19, 22, 24, 25, 26, 27, 28, 29, 30, 31, 32, 33, 34, 35, 36, 38, 39, 42, 43, 44 and 45.

9. There is an effective parallelism in τοῦ πλούτου τῆς χρηστότητος...καταφρονεῖς (items 16 and 19) and ἀγνοῶν ὅτι τὸ χρηστὸν τοῦ θεοῦ (items 20-21).

10. The reinforcing of the same concept by repetition of different expressions is effective in τὴν σκληρότητά σου and ἀμετανόητον καρδίαν in items 23 and 24.

11. Figurative expressions are effectively employed in ἐκφεύξῃ 'will escape' and θησαυρίζεις 'treasure up' (items 14 and 25).

12. The parallel expressions in items 40 and 41 heigh-ten the distinction in meaning. Likewise the pa-rallel references to Jews and Greeks, though in a shift of case, also add emphasis.

13. Toward the end of this passage there is a signifi-cant increase in the amount of ellipsis. Note items 33, 34, 38, 42, 43, and 44.

14. It is possible that the rather long sentence (items 29-38) becomes unmanageable syntactically, and therefore a new start has to begin with item 39. Nevertheless the juxtaposition of ὀργὴ καὶ θυμός and θλῖψις καὶ στενοχωρία (items 38 and 39) is certainly effective as a transitional device.

15. There is a significant chiastic structure in the thematic development. Benefits are noted in items 32-34, but punishment is implied in items 35-38. Immediately after the anacoluthon, punishments are again noted in items 39-40, while benefits and blessings are listed in items 41-44.

16. In items 36 and 37 there is an interesting shift

in negation so as to make possible parallel expressions which reinforce one another, but which
are negative in a type of chiastic shift in the
negative prefix α-. Compare ἀπειθοῦσι τῇ ἀληθείᾳ
'those disobeying the truth' in contrast with
πειθομένοις δὲ τῇ ἀδικίᾳ 'but obeying injustice'.

17. There is one rhetorical question in this series
(namely, items 10-15).

In the analysis of narrative, one must adopt a quite different procedure. Though there are, of course, the same basic
relationships between nuclear structures, these are not as
important as a recognition of the episodic developments.
Therefore, narrative is best treated as a scenario of
events, but in order to analyze narrative satisfactorily, it
is important to take into consideration all of the basic
elements, including participants, relationship between participants, relevant objects, the sequence of events (whether
pivotal or nonpivotal), rhetorical features, semantic features, and especially matters of setting, including textual
setting, communicative setting, and cultural setting. Only
then can one satisfactorily deal with problems of symbolic
or higher-level meaning in the case of parables.

In order to illustrate some of the significant factors
involved in narrative structures, the story of the Prodigal
Son has been selected, since it is the most complex of the
short narratives.

Luke 15.11-32:   11 Εἶπεν δέ· ἄνθρωπός τις εἶχεν δύο υἱούς. 12 καὶ εἶπεν
ὁ νεώτερος αὐτῶν τῷ πατρί· πάτερ, δός μοι τὸ ἐπιβάλλον
μέρος τῆς οὐσίας. ὁ δὲ διεῖλεν αὐτοῖς τὸν βίον. 13 καὶ
μετ' οὐ πολλὰς ἡμέρας συναγαγὼν πάντα ὁ νεώτερος
υἱὸς ἀπεδήμησεν εἰς χώραν μακρὰν καὶ ἐκεῖ διεσκόρπισεν
τὴν οὐσίαν αὐτοῦ ζῶν ἀσώτως. 14 δαπανήσαντος δὲ
αὐτοῦ πάντα ἐγένετο λιμὸς ἰσχυρὰ κατὰ τὴν χώραν ἐκεί-
νην, καὶ αὐτὸς ἤρξατο ὑστερεῖσθαι. 15 καὶ πορευθεὶς
ἐκολλήθη ἑνὶ τῶν πολιτῶν τῆς χώρας ἐκείνης, καὶ ἔπεμ-
ψεν αὐτὸν εἰς τοὺς ἀγροὺς αὐτοῦ βόσκειν χοίρους, 16 καὶ
ἐπεθύμει χορτασθῆναι ἐκ τῶν κερατίων ὧν ἤσθιον οἱ

χοῖροι, καὶ οὐδεὶς ἐδίδου αὐτῷ. 17 εἰς ἑαυτὸν δὲ ἐλθὼν
ἔφη· πόσοι μίσθιοι τοῦ πατρός μου περισσεύονται ἄρ-
των, ἐγὼ δὲ λιμῷ ὧδε ἀπόλλυμαι. 18 ἀναστὰς πορεύσο-
μαι πρὸς τὸν πατέρα μου καὶ ἐρῶ αὐτῷ· πάτερ, ἥμαρτον
εἰς τὸν οὐρανὸν καὶ ἐνώπιόν σου, 19 οὐκέτι εἰμὶ ἄξιος
κληθῆναι υἱός σου· ποίησόν με ὡς ἕνα τῶν μισθίων σου.
20 καὶ ἀναστὰς ἦλθεν πρὸς τὸν πατέρα ἑαυτοῦ. Ἔτι
δὲ αὐτοῦ μακρὰν ἀπέχοντος εἶδεν αὐτὸν ὁ πατὴρ αὐτοῦ
καὶ ἐσπλαγχνίσθη καὶ δραμὼν ἐπέπεσεν ἐπὶ τὸν τράχη-
λον αὐτοῦ καὶ κατεφίλησεν αὐτόν. 21 εἶπεν δὲ ὁ υἱὸς
αὐτῷ · πάτερ, ἥμαρτον εἰς τὸν οὐρανὸν καὶ ἐνώπιόν σου,
οὐκέτι εἰμὶ ἄξιος κληθῆναι υἱός σου . 22 εἶπεν δὲ ὁ πατὴρ πρὸς τοὺς δούλους αὐτοῦ· ταχὺ ἐξενέγκατε στο-
λὴν τὴν πρώτην καὶ ἐνδύσατε αὐτόν, καὶ δότε δακτύλιον
εἰς τὴν χεῖρα αὐτοῦ καὶ ὑποδήματα εἰς τοὺς πόδας, 23 καὶ
φέρετε τὸν μόσχον τὸν σιτευτόν, θύσατε, καὶ φαγόντες
εὐφρανθῶμεν, 24 ὅτι οὗτος ὁ υἱός μου νεκρὸς ἦν καὶ ἀν-
έζησεν, ἦν ἀπολωλὼς καὶ εὑρέθη. καὶ ἤρξαντο εὐ-
φραίνεσθαι. 25 Ἦν δὲ ὁ υἱὸς αὐτοῦ ὁ πρεσβύτερος
ἐν ἀγρῷ· καὶ ὡς ἐρχόμενος ἤγγισεν τῇ οἰκίᾳ, ἤκουσεν
συμφωνίας καὶ χορῶν, 26 καὶ προσκαλεσάμενος ἕνα τῶν
παίδων ἐπυνθάνετο τί ἂν εἴη ταῦτα . 27 ὁ δὲ εἶπεν αὐτῷ
ὅτι ὁ ἀδελφός σου ἥκει, καὶ ἔθυσεν ὁ πατήρ σου τὸν
μόσχον τὸν σιτευτόν, ὅτι ὑγιαίνοντα αὐτὸν ἀπέλαβεν.
28 ὠργίσθη δὲ καὶ οὐκ ἤθελεν εἰσελθεῖν, ὁ δὲ πατὴρ αὐτοῦ ἐξελθὼν παρεκάλει αὐτόν. 29 ὁ δὲ ἀποκριθεὶς εἶπεν
τῷ πατρὶ ⁰αὐτοῦ· ἰδοὺ τοσαῦτα ἔτη δουλεύω σοι καὶ
οὐδέποτε ἐντολήν σου παρῆλθον, καὶ ἐμοὶ οὐδέποτε ἔδω-
κας ἔριφον ἵνα μετὰ τῶν φίλων μου εὐφρανθῶ· 30 ὅτε
δὲ ὁ υἱός σου οὗτος ὁ καταφαγών σου τὸν βίον μετὰ
πορνῶν ἦλθεν, ἔθυσας αὐτῷ τὸν σιτευτὸν μόσχον.
31 ὁ δὲ εἶπεν αὐτῷ· τέκνον, σὺ πάντοτε μετ' ἐμοῦ εἶ, καὶ
πάντα τὰ ἐμὰ σά ἐστιν· 32 εὐφρανθῆναι δὲ καὶ χαρῆναι
ἔδει, ὅτι ὁ ἀδελφός σου οὗτος νεκρὸς ἦν καὶ ἔζησεν, καὶ
ἀπολωλὼς καὶ εὑρέθη.

A translation of this passage in the Today's English Version
may be useful in following the descriptive analysis:

[11]Jesus went on to say, "There was once a man who had two
sons. [12]The younger one said to him, 'Father, give me my
share of the property now.' So the man divided his property
between his two sons. [13]After a few days the younger son
sold his part of the property and left home with the money.
He went to a country far away, where he wasted his money in
reckless living. [14]He spent everything he had. Then a se-

vere famine spread over that country, and he was left without a thing. ¹⁵So he went to work for one of the citizens of that country, who sent him out to his farm to take care of the pigs. ¹⁶He wished he could fill himself with the bean pods the pigs ate, but no one gave him anything to eat. ¹⁷At last he came to his senses and said, 'All my father's hired workers have more than they can eat, and here I am about to starve! ¹⁸I will get up and go to my father and say, "Father, I have sinned against God and against you. ¹⁹I am no longer fit to be called your son; treat me as one of your hired workers".' ²⁰So he got up and started back to his father.

"He was still a long way from home when his father saw him; his heart was filled with pity, and he ran, threw his arms around his son, and kissed him. ²¹'Father', the son said, 'I have sinned against God and against you. I am no longer fit to be called your son.' ²²But the father called to his servants. 'Hurry!' he said. 'Bring the best robe and put it on him. Put a ring on his finger and shoes on his feet. ²³Then go and get the prize calf and kill it, and let us celebrate with a feast! ²⁴For this son of mine was dead, but now he is alive; he was lost, but now he has been found.' And so the feasting began.

²⁵"In the meantime the older son was out in the field. On his way back, when he came close to the house, he heard the music and dancing. ²⁶So he called one of the servants and asked him, 'What's going on?' ²⁷'Your brother has come back home', the servant answered, 'and your father has killed the prize calf, because he got him back safe and sound'. ²⁸The older brother was so angry that he would not go into the house; so his father came out and begged him to come in. ²⁹But he spoke back to his father, 'Look, all these years I have worked for you like a slave, and I have never disobeyed your orders. What have you given me? Not even a goat for me to have a feast with my friends! ³⁰But this son of yours

wasted all your property on prostitutes, and when he comes back home, you kill the prize calf for him!' [31]'My son', the father answered, 'you are always here with me, and everything I have is yours. [32]But we had to celebrate and be happy, because your brother was dead, but now he is alive; he was lost, but now he has been found'."

The participants consist of two sets, principal and non-principal. The father, the younger son, and the older son constitute the principal persons whose actions and decisions are pivotal for the narrative sequence. The foreign land-owner and the servants participate only as circumstancial adjuncts. Their actions as such do not significantly determine the development of the story sequence.

The basic relationship between the principal participants is a triple dyadic one, that is to say, there is a two way relationship between father and younger son, father and older son, and younger son and older son. This results in a type of triadic structure.

The relevant objects in this narrative consist of the property which was divided, the prize calf, and the garment, shoes, and ring.

The scenario of events is divided into two series, the first concerns primarily the younger son, and the second, the older son. Within the series one must also note the difference between pivotal and nonpivotal events. Pivotal events are those decisions/actions which significantly change the narrative direction of the story. Nonpivotal events are those which are essentially derivatives of such pivotal events. In the following listing of the series of events, the two series are distinguished and are numbered, and the pivotal events are those with an asterisk.

Series 1

1	*2	3	4	5
request for inheritance	division of property	turned into cash	far country	wasted

6	*7	8	9	10	*11
famine	need	work for foreigner	care of pigs	eat pig food	comes to self

12	*13	14	15	16
returns home	father accepts	father orders clothes, shoes, ring	father orders festival	festival takes place

Series 2

*17	18	19	20	21
older brother arrives	aware of festival	asks servant	learns reason	refuses to enter

*22	23	24	25
father comes out	older son objects	father explains older son's status	father defends festival

This story of the Prodigal Son can perhaps better be called 'The Parable of the Two Sons' or possibly 'The Parable of Lost and Found'. It is remarkable indeed how much meaning has been packed into a very brief narrative structure.

In terms of rhetorical features, it is interesting to note that there is little or no description. No psychological explanations are given, and the only statements of emotion are to be found in the pity which the father has for his younger son when he returns, and the angry reaction of the older brother. All the meaning of this story is to be found in words and deeds. There is of course the dominant theme of "lost, found, and celebration" (also found in the preceding two parables) which gives significant unity to the first sequence of events, and there is the emphatic repetition of the themes "dead and alive" and "lost and found", which occurs in verses 24 and 32, in the first instance, completing series 1, and in the second instance, completing series 2.

At crucial points in the story, direct discourse is effectively employed, for example, in items 1, 11, 12, 13, 20, 23, 24, and 25.

It is interesting that the younger son in each case addresses his father with πάτερ, while the older son does not use any such expression of polite address, though the father does respond to his older son with τέκνον, equivalent to 'my child' or 'my son'.

There are a number of brief but well placed transitional devices consisting primarily of temporal and spatial setting; for example, μετ' οὐ πολλὰς ἡμέρας 'after not many days' (verse 13), ἔτι δὲ αὐτοῦ μακρὰν ἀπέχοντος 'while still quite a way off' (verse 20), καὶ ὡς ἐρχόμενος ἤγγισεν τῇ οἰκίᾳ 'and as he came near to the house...' (verse 25).

The semantic structure of this narrative reflects several significant contrasts. For example, the younger son sins and then repents, while the older son does not sin but is unforgiving. The younger son gets possession of his inheritance but wastes it, while the older son also gets possession but never enjoys it. In a sense, he does not really enter into his inheritance. As a third contrast, one may say that the younger son distances himself from his father but returns, while the older son stays with the father, but in reality distances himself emotionally from his father as well as from his brother. It is also significant that the father refuses to intrude into the lives of his sons. He could have sent servants into the far country to rescue his younger son whom he no doubt knew would soon be in trouble. Evidently the father also assumes that the older son should decide for himself when he wishes to make a feast for some of his friends.

In understanding the meaning of this parable, it is essential to look at three different aspects of the setting, the textual, the communicative, and the cultural. In the textual setting the parable of the prodigal son is the third in a series of three parables, all dealing with the same theme of lost-found-celebration. Moreover, in the first two parables the joy of the celebration is likened to what takes place in heaven when a sinner repents. Such a theological conclusion hardly seems necessary at the end of the story of the Prodigal Son. In the first two parables, it is the property which has been lost and found, but in the third parable, the property of the younger son is lost but the son is found, while the property of the older son is not lost, but the older son is 'lost'. In this connection it is significant that the parable is open-ended, that is to say, all the problems are not resolved, for there is no indication that the older son repents of his self-righteous attitude.

The communicative setting of this parable also helps to highlight its significance, for in the communicative setting there is likewise a triad of participants: Jesus, his followers, and the Pharisees and scribes. Moreover, there is a dyadic relationship between the three sets in the triad: Jesus speaks to his disciples who hear him gladly and who have repented. The Pharisees, on the other hand, listen to Jesus but are hostile toward what he says and are unrepentant. Furthermore, the Pharisees are hostile toward the followers of Jesus whom they regard as condemned by God since they do not practice the requirements of the Law. The significance of this triad of persons in the communicative setting is highlighted at the beginning of Luke 15. The tax collectors and outcasts came near to listen to Jesus, while the Pharisees and the scribes murmured against Jesus for receiving and eating with religious outcasts.

Elements in the cultural setting also help to highlight certain features of the narrative. For example, the fact that

property in this case would have been divided one-third to
the younger son and two-thirds to the older son was in keeping with the Jewish practice of giving to the firstborn son
twice as much as any other offspring would receive. The
fact that the younger son had to go to work for a foreigner
would have been degrading, but to have been given the task
of herding swine and even wanting to eat the food the swine
ate was as low in status as any Jew could have fallen.

The three items requested for the younger son by the father,
namely, the clothes, shoes, and ring, probably had highly
symbolic significance. The ring, at least, went far beyond
the physical need of the younger son and would no doubt have
symbolized clearly to all his continuing as a true member of
the family. To heighten the significance of the return of
the younger son, the festival was completely appropriate and
meaningful.

Because of the analogical relationships between the triad of
persons in the communicative setting and the triad of participants in the narrative itself, it is not difficult to see
the relationships. The younger son would certainly represent those repentant persons who responded to the Good News
of God's love. The older son would no doubt represent the
religious hardliners of the day, namely the Pharisees and
scribes, whose legalism made it difficult for them to be
forgiving. The father no doubt represents the attitude of
God in accepting repentant outcasts and proclaiming a joyous
festival, something which is certainly implied also in the
two previous parables.

CHAPTER 9

The Communication Process

In order to understand various implications of the communication process, it is important to bear constantly in mind the fundamental relationship between the three essential factors in any communication, namely, the source, the message, and the receptors. Ideally, one would hope that the decoding of any communication by receptors would be simply the converse of the encoding process, so that the result of the communication process would reflect essential identity of meaning. This is, however, never the case, since no two people share completely the same backgrounds, have identical value systems, or operate on the basis of completely equivalent sets of presuppositions. The essential problems of communication usually increase proportionate to the differences in cultures, particularly as such cultures may have very different presuppositions about ultimate reality and quite distinct value systems.

Though communication often appears to be relatively simple in the relationship between source, message, and receptor, there are always a number of complicating factors. In oral communication one must always reckon with paralinguistic features of the verbal code, namely, intonation, quality of voice, volume, relative pitch, rapidity of speech, enunciation, and pronunciation. All of these paralinguistic features provide important clues as to the background of the speaker, his emotional state, his involvement in the subject matter, and his attitude toward receptors. In addition to the paralinguistic features, one must also reckon with extralinguistic features, particularly gestures, body stance, muscle tone, facial expressions, and general appearance. The communication setting of time and place can also contribute considerably to the interpretation of a statement. Even a statement such as <u>damn it</u> may have differences of denotation and particularly of connotation, depending upon where it is uttered, in a classroom, office, church, home, or at a ballgame.

Written communication is far more limited in paralinguistic and extralinguistic features. The lack of a well-defined communication setting and the absence of clearly marked interpersonal relations seem to contribute to what many regard as the "independent existence of written texts". In a number of circumstances the author of a written text is not known, the circumstances of the writing may be a mystery, and the reader may not care about such matters. In fact, the circumstances of the original production of a text may be so completely different from the circumstances in which a text is read that a comparison between the two settings would be completely irrelevant. Nevertheless, there are certain factors in the written form of a text which do contribute significantly to its interpretation. Correctness of orthographic details (numerous misprints in a text certainly have a negative connotative value), the format (old-fashioned page formats are often associated with old-fashioned ideas), the quality of printing, and even the binding of a book signal a good deal about the nature of the message.

Though the problem of noise, whether physical or psychological, is clearly evident in oral communication, there is a sense in which the factor of "noise" enters into the problem of transmission of texts, for noise, in terms of communication theory, is anything which distorts or obscures the form of the text during the process of communication. In the case of the Bible, there are a number of problems of such noise, including especially the transition from oral tradition to written text and from the original autographs to existing manuscripts on which critical texts can be based.

In oral communication there is an important factor of feedback. It may take the form of heckling, booing, or applause, but it is often far more subtle and expressed by lack of attention, failure to maintain eye contact, and antagonistic facial gestures. Unfortunately, written communication does not permit this kind of feedback, though one often does have a record of the way in which those who received the original message responded to it, either by praise or criticism. On the other hand, there is one aspect of feedback which is particularly important, namely, anticipatory feedback, the way in which an author anticipates the probable reactions of his receptors and thus organizes his message to meet those objections. If this is structured in a formal and explicit way, the resulting literary genre is called diatribe (compare 1 Corinthians 15.12-58).

One of the important ways in which a person may evaluate the significance or relevance of a text is to determine the evident communicative function which it was intended to fulfill. The eight basic communicative functions have already been discussed in Chapter 2, but for the Scriptures, the most important of these functions are the informative, imperative, performative, and emotive functions. Rarely is any one discourse directed at only one function , but it is often possible to determine the function by studying the background data relevant to any communication (who said what to whom, for what purpose and under what circumstances), the literary genre, the style, and the content as a basis for determining various degrees of urgency, concern, or importance as signalled by various stylistic devices.

The interpretative process in understanding a text consists essentially of three major aspects: (1) the perception of a sign or group of related signs, (2) the integrated evaluation of the various codes, and (3) the determination of the referent or referents.

The perception of signs is essentially a psychological phenomenon received by the various senses and then registered in the cognitive process.

The second stage is far more complex, for it must involve the integrated approach to the various codes in order to determine the contribution which the various codes make to the overall meaning.

The language code may perhaps be best described in terms of three subcodes: lexical, syntactic, and rhetorical. The lexical subcode consists of primarily words and idioms, though in some instances bound morphemes and phonetic symbolism may be relevant. The syntactic subcode is essentially a matter of combinatory meaning and involves nuclear structures (often called kernels), clauses, sentences, and overt reference marking between sentences.

The rhetorical structures (as described in chapter 2) may be said to involve meaningful "patterns", marked sometimes by single features but more often by a collection of features.

As already noted, the accompanying codes are primarily paralinguistic and extralinguistic, but in some instances one must also reckon with a continuous accompanying code such as music or acting. Certainly in drama the action that accompanies the verbal message is highly significant in the interpretation of what is said. The same is also true for songs in which the music itself may indicate whether the words are to be understood, for example, in a romantic or an erotic sense.

In order to obtain important hints with regard to the relative significance of the language subcodes and the accompanying codes, it is indispensable to examine the settings: textual, communicative, and cultural.

In the case of an embedded discourse unit, it is essential to examine the contiguous portions of the total text in order to see precisely what may have contributed to the embedding of a unit at the particular place, for usually what precedes and follows provides an important hint as to relevance. One may also examine other texts prepared by the same author in order to evaluate various aspects of the verbal code, and even the examination of the same themes and structures in other discourses (the area of intertextuality) may be valuable. This is particularly true for the New Testament when so much can be derived from a comparison of the Greek New Testament with the Septuagint translation of the Old Testament.

The communicative setting in terms of who communicated to whom, when, where, and how also provides important insights, but the communicative setting is often on two quite different levels: external and internal. The external communicative setting involves the circumstances in which a source prepared a text for a particular constituency. The internal setting involves any account of a particular discourse unit within a larger text. The parable of the Good Samaritan, for example, receives its significance from the internal communicative setting.

The cultural setting can also provide very significant information with regard to elements within a discourse. For the New Testament world, the ease of divorce, the widespread practice of slavery, male dominance, ethnoreligious prejudice (particularly between Jews and Samaritans and between Jews and Gentiles) and the clash of ideologies and cultures are all factors which contribute to an evaluation of the various codes.

In determining the referent of any discourse, one must look at all the relevant levels, from the smallest to the largest units. The smallest unit which is propositionally significant is usually a single sentence, but in some instances single sentences are so closely integrated into a paragraph, that the paragraph itself may be the most relevant minimal unit. Beyond the paragraph, however, one must deal with sections, chapters, and entire discourses. These various units may be related to one another in a number of ways. The various semantic relations have already been discussed in Chapter 7. The three principal structural relationships between units of a text consist of hierarchies, chains (series of linked units), and circles or spirals, that is to say, series which ultimately turn back upon themselves but which may be related to one another on a higher level.

One may also view the relationship between units of a text (whether these units are thematic or structural) in terms of sets of similarities or contrasts. Traditionally, these have been analyzed usually in terms of binary contrasts, for example, life/death, joy/sadness, hero/antihero, protagonist/antagonist, progression/regression, real/unreal, true/false. It would be wrong, however, to assume that one must always find binary contrasts. Relationships may also be trinary, and relationships need not be contrastive but may be reinforcing by both similarity and analogy.

The interpretive process may also involve three degrees of involvement as specified by Charles Peirce in terms of firstness, secondness, and thirdness. Firstness consists of the immediate sensory, prereflective response or reaction to a text. One's immediate emotive reaction to hearing a symphony would be regarded as a first level of understanding. The same would apply to the story of the Good Samaritan, when a person first hears it read and is attracted to the quality of the story.

Secondness in interpreting a discourse would involve awareness of time, space, content, and structure. It would consist of what one sees in the text and thus reckons with the singularity of the signs. As one listens to a symphony, for example, one might be fully aware of the composer, the time at which the symphony was composed, and something about its internal structure. Similarly, in reading the story of the Good Samaritan, one might be fully aware of the communicative setting and the evident intent of the parable as an answer to ethnocentrism.

The third level of the interpretive process would concentrate upon what one sees through such a text. It would involve a generalization of the implication of such a discourse, and the implication of this for other signs. The analogy with listening to a symphony would mean not only appreciating the particular symphony but understanding the history of music and those elements of musicology which entered into the symphony. Furthermore, one would need to appreciate the influence which such a symphony has had upon later musical productions. By comparison, a study of the parable of the Good Samaritan would reveal something more than the implication of the story for the audience to whom it was originally spoken. It would contribute significantly to our understanding of Luke's concern for justice, interpersonal relations to foreigners, and in a sense, an anticipatory account of the spread of the Gospel as recorded in the book of Acts, first to Samaria and then to other parts of the Greco-Roman world.

In a sense, the various levels of interpretive involvement parallel the distinction between exegesis and hermeneutics (although these terms are sometimes used interchangably). However, it is often useful to make a clear distinction. Exegesis would then consist in reconstructing the original communication event in terms of source, message, receptors, communicative setting, cultural background, and immediately subsequent influence of the communication. Hermeneutics, on the other hand, would involve the transfer of the meaning of such a discourse into an entirely different time-space context. Hence, drawing the implications of the story of the Good Samaritan to circumstances of the present day would involve hermeneutics, while determining the meaning of such an account in its original setting would be exegesis.

CHAPTER 10

Literature and Its Study

Despite the enormous time and effort expended on the study and appreciation of literature, there is no general agreement as to what are the necessary and sufficient features of a discourse to make it an example of literature. Since the definition of literature would inevitably involve some evaluation and since the value systems of cultures are subject to considerable change, it is no wonder that what may be regarded as first-rate literature in one century can be thought to be relatively banal discourse in another. The same is true, of course, of all artistic endeavor. What one generation may regard as cacophonous noise another generation may accept as music.

Rather than attempt to determine the nature of literature by means of certain necessary and sufficient features which might be valid for all time, it is no doubt best to regard literature as consisting of a family or cluster of features which tend to be present in varying degrees in what might be called "significant texts". Such texts would no doubt involve a significant theme, usually of existential relevance, and would be effectively structured so as to provide both impact and appeal for important insights on various levels.

As Roman Jakobson (1960) has pointed out, one crucial feature of literature results from the effect of the poetic function which projects "the principle of equivalence from the axis of selection to the axis of combination". In general, this means that one selects a theme, employs a number of motifs, organizes the text in terms of a particular genre and incorporates those rhetorical or stylistic features which will appropriately highlight various aspects of the message. For example, one may wish to treat the theme of life/death. To do this, several different motifs might be employed, for example, youth/old age, spring/fall, and blooming/wilting. Any one of several genres might be employed, for example, a poem, a short story, a novel, a proverb, or a biography. The rhetorical features employed in the development of such a theme would depend largely upon the genre and the acceptability of such features for the presumed audience of such a message.

In the Gospel of John the twin themes of acceptance/rejection and suffering/exaltation seem to dominate, while the motifs are signs, growing opposition, and a failure of people to understand the spiritual rather than the literal significance of Jesus' words. The genre may very well be regarded as "dramatic history" or "dramatic biography".

There are always special problems involved with religious language, and this is particularly true in connection with the New Testament. In the treatment of religious language one must make a clear distinction between primary religious language, that is to say, the language of the original validating documents or utterances and secondary religious language, that is to say, the kind of language which develops at a later stage and is essentially dependent upon primary language. Such distinctions between primary and secondary religious language exist in the case of all religions, but the following discussion will be restricted to the primary and secondary religious language of Christianity in view of the focus of this volume, namely, the style and discourse of the Greek New Testament.

(1) Primary religious language tends to make extensive use of figurative expressions. Any attempt to relate infinite realities to finite experience almost inevitably calls for figurative language, since there are no natural models which combine infinite and finite elements. In order to reach beyond the time/space limitations of human experience, primary religious language has to grasp the significance of

supernatural realities by means of radical figurative expressions.

(2) Primary religious language tends to employ a historical framework in order to validate its tradition, but one must not expect such documentation to be the equivalent of court reporting. The often ecstatic exaltation of direct religious experience is existentially so timeless as to not seem to require a rigid historical perspective.

(3) Primary religious language employs a number of rather highly technical expressions, usually of a figurative nature, for example, in the New Testament such phrases as 'saved by his blood', 'in the heavenlies', 'emptied himself', 'the Word became flesh', 'baptism of the Spirit', and 'believe and obey'.

(4) Primary religious language also employs a great deal of instructional material, usually in the form of regulations and laws, but these are usually not systematically organized into any code. Rather, they are the practical expression of the life of the community as it faces internal and external problems and relations.

(5) Primary religious language is conspicuous by its lack of apologetic and defensive utterances. In this respect it contrasts radically with secondary religious language. Evidently, those who participate in the primary religious context are so overwhelmed with the reality of what they feel and do that it seems superfluous to try to defend the experience.

(6) Primary religious language normally contains a great deal of appeal for commitment, either on the part of the in-group or as a potential instrument for appealing to members of an out-group.

(7) Primary religious language normally revolves around personalities, both human and divine. It is the experience of individuals which captures the attention of others. The focus is upon supernatural events and human response rather than upon a system of thought.

In contrast with primary religious language, secondary religious language exhibits a number of strikingly different but complementary features: (1) the frequent repetition of figurative and/or technical expressions, but largely for group identification and validation, (2) numerous technical expressions related to the tendency to explain or defend dogma, for example, realized eschatology, kerygma, Heilsgeschichte, (3) extensive explanatory texts, which normally follow or are dependent upon the dominant philosophical system of any one epoch or period, (4) systematic codification of rules, doctrines, and beliefs, and (5) finally, a tendency to demythologize some of the more striking and less well understood figurative language. Demythologizing is presumably done for the sake of the out-group, but in reality probably more appreciated by in-group members who have become intellectually disenchanted with some of the imponderables of the primary religious language.

In any religious community there are inevitably certain significant results which derive from problems involved in the nature of primary religious texts. Though seeming inconsistencies and contradictions in primary religious texts do not bother people who are close to the source in time or in emotional identity, these do become serious problems for people in later generations. In many instances these lead to extravagant explanations, as may be readily witnessed by some of the attempts to explain differences in the synoptics, or to justify Old Testament quotations from the Septuagint rather than from Hebrew, or to reconcile some of the differences in statistics between 1 and 2 Kings and 1 and 2 Chronicles.

Probably the most significant effect of primary religious language upon later developments relates to the abundance of figurative language, originally designed to explain the supernatural elements of religious experience. In later generations, however, such figurative language is often subject to literalist interpretation, as in the case of such phrases as "Son of God", "gehenna of fire", and "this is my blood". Because some figurative language is not understood clearly, it acquires a kind of mystic aura, and this tends to lead to what may be regarded as "word idolatry", so that there is a tendency to read into words meaning and values which are really foreign to the primary religious usage.

Jews and Christians have always hesitated to look upon their Holy Scriptures as being merely literature, and accordingly there is a tendency to avoid attempts to speak of the Bible as "great literature". Such attitudes are justified in view of the crucial importance attached to the unique supernatural events recorded in the Holy Scriptures. Nevertheless, it is impossible to avoid completely the implications of literary analysis when speaking of the Bible. To do so would ultimately rob the Scriptures of much of their dynamic significance. In fact, an appreciation of the literary qualities of the biblical texts can only lead to a greater appreciation of their relevance. It is therefore important to see the study of the literary features of the Bible in terms of various approaches to literature. In the following brief review of certain major tendencies in the study of literary texts, it is impossible to treat all or even most of the significant contributions to literary analysis. However, it may be useful to sketch at least some of the broader outlines of these developments, particularly in relation to what has happened during the last fifty years, in which insights from linguistics, anthropology, psychology, semantics, and semiotics have made so many contributions to our understanding and appreciation of the various structures and features.

In general, one may divide the various approaches to literature as involving two distinct orientations: (1) developmental (including psychological), with a focus upon the author or authors, and (2) the "text as text", without concern for the historical contexts which have contributed to the form of a text.

The developmental approach to literature may also be subdivided between a focus upon the psychological and the sociological factors which contribute to the development. For the New Testament, certainly the psychological element of inspiration has been a dominant orientation. Some persons would even go so far as to suggest a kind of dictation approach to the formation of the biblical text, even claiming at times that the Greek of the New Testament is a kind of "Holy Ghost language". Other persons would simply insist that the authors wrote better than they knew, and despite the fact of being human, they were kept from error.

Other approaches of a psychological nature have focused upon the creativity of the author's contribution to a literary text. This aspect has been particularly important in the study of the works of "literary geniuses", and a great deal has been written to try to explain why and how authors such as Shakespeare, Dante, Milton, and Goethe were able to produce such masterpieces. A number of scholars inevitably turned to Freudianism to explain creativity and to show how most writing is unconsciously auto-biographical. This enthusiasm for psychological explanation has, however, largely waned within the last few years.

A sociological explanation of literature has been widespread and particularly favored by a number of biblical scholars who see the New Testament as being the result of the experience of the believing community. This approach focuses upon the manner in which the text grew by stages and underwent varying degrees of recension and redaction. A Marxist approach to literature has clearly been dialectical in orientation, with attempts to chart the relationship between social movements and literary developments, even to the point of seeing analogies between social structures and literary patterns.

Increasingly, however, modern approaches to literature have focused upon the "text as text", without attempting to explain its development, since in so many instances the evidence is scanty, and even in cases in which authors are still living, their descriptions of the creative processes are often both obscure and evidently misleading. However, to treat the text as text, two major approaches have been employed: (1) thematic and ideational, and (2) structural.

The thematic or ideational approach to the study of a text has focused upon themes, motifs, unfolding relations, factors of progression and coherence, diversity and unity, heroes and antiheroes, and protagonists and antagonists.

More recently, however, the shift has been more toward a structural analysis. The so-called "New Criticism" of the University of Chicago led the way in cutting off the study of literature from its developmental orientation. The focus was upon structure as the basis for revealing meaning. The atemporal and autonomous nature of any literary text was emphasized, and considerable progress was made in focusing upon structural features which had often been overlooked in the past.

The contribution of the French anthropologist Lévi-Strauss (1951) fits in well into this structural orientation, but Lévi-Strauss went somewhat further in emphasizing the deterministic aspect of the processes of thought and therefore of literature. Taking his clue from the phonology of the Prague school of linguistics, he made an extensive study of (1) different forms of the same myths and (2) similar myths in different parts of the world (particularly the western hemisphere). In these he found a number of analogous and contrastive features which he set up in terms of binary sets of meaningful contrasts, though he attached to certain contrasts far more importance than to others, for example, kinship and sex. He was really not concerned if the sets of contrasts seemed relevant to the people from whom he obtained the myths. He insisted that the contrasts were valid on a subliminal level, even if not on a conscious level. The appeal of such an approach to some biblical scholars can be readily understood.

The semantic structuralist approach is associated primarily with the name of Greimas (1966), who gave great emphasis to binary contrasts of primarily positive and negative dimensions. He saw in all words a kind of basic underlying meaning consisting of certain fundamental semes (minimal units of meaning), and these he put into classes of semes which he called classemes, though the precise methodology for this type of classification was not worked out in any rigorous detail. Greimas has not been concerned essentially with the communicative context but rather with any and all possible contrasts which might exist within a text. Greimas was not concerned with any built-in system to determine the relevance of such differences. In contrast with Greimas, Umberto Eco (1979) would insist upon the communicative context as being the basis for any valid semantic or semiological study of communication or meaning.

Derrida (1967) has taken an even more radical approach than other structuralists in not only isolating a text from its communicative source but also from other texts. He would regard each creative piece of literature as constituting its own model. Underlying each and all literary texts there is for Derrida a so-called "geno-text", but the geno-text is too abstract to define all the ways in which derivative pheno-texts develop from it. On the other hand, a great deal of meaning is derived from cultural contexts based upon various conventions, themes, and models.

One of the most recent and perhaps productive approaches to the study of literature is to be found in the work of an increasing number of scholars concerned with a comparative approach to literature. This involves concern for what is called "intertextuality", but this means not only similar texts within the same language but similar texts in all languages having a literature, whether oral or written. Persons concerned with the comparative approach are obviously looking for universal features of literature as a means of understanding and appreciating both the similarities and the differences to be found in literary productions in languages throughout the world.

In order to understand something of the nature of literature, it is also necessary to be clear about the relationship of language to literature. Literature makes use of languages as the raw material. In the same way that a potter employs clay to produce an object of ceramic art, so an author employs the raw material of language to produce literature. This means that a literary text is in certain respects richer than language, though of course it is not as extensive. The particular patterns of rhetorical structure which mold the raw material of language into a particular form produce an object of both cultural relevance and esthetic value.

Literary texts provide information, but they also, in a sense, create information, for they suggest new insights on several levels, and the imaginative character of such information inevitably leads to a variety of interpretations. This is true of any masterfully composed esthetic object. Its meaning for an audience may go far beyond what was intended by the one who produced it.

In view of the intimate relationship between language and literature, it seems quite clear that language actually is the best tool for the analysis of literature. In the first place, it is the one code of sufficient complexity to have a metalinguistic function, that is to say, language is a code which can be used to speak about itself. Furthermore, it is by far the most complex code. But perhaps what makes it particularly important for the study of literature is that it is open-ended, that is to say, it is a code which has an almost infinite capacity for expansion and modification. At the same time language is a code which mirrors and reflects the real world. In this there are a number of severe limitations, for no language is an exact reproduction of the thoughts, feelings, and patterns of behavior of a society. Nevertheless, language is better in this respect than any other code.

Though language is a highly significant instrument for dealing with the nature of literature, it is too restricted to take into consideration all the symbolic elements of communication. It is for this reason that a more comprehensive science of signs is required, and this is precisely why the approach of this volume has been semiotic in orientation. From the standpoint of the relationship between language and literature, semiotics is crucial for several reasons. In the first place, it takes the referents of language seriously. It is not restricted, as Saussure's system of signifier and signified has proven to be. Language is far more than an oral and/or mental phenomenon, for language brings one in touch with the real world of sensory experience.

In the second place, semiotics relates denotative meaning to referents. In fact, the referents are given priority, so that meaning (in dictionary terms) is abstracted from the communicative events. Meaning, accordingly, is derivative of referents rather than the reverse. This is certainly true for any child learning to speak a language. His growing understanding of the meaning of verbal signs results from his awareness of how such signs are used in connection with particular referents. Furthermore, dictionary definitions themselves are largely based upon those features of referents which provide clues to the meaning and hence the referential potential of any verbal sign.

In the third place, semiotics provides insight into the manner in which connotations are largely derived from the circumstances of who uses what sign, when, where, under what circumstances, and for what evident purpose. The connotative meaning of the so-called "four-letter words" is an obvious case of semiotic significance based upon setting.

In the fourth place, semiotics clearly shows how signs can be defined only by other signs. This means that within any code signs are defined negatively by virtue of the fact that they contrast with or are limited by other signs. But semiotics also provides a way of understanding how, in addition to the linguistic contrasts which exist within any language code, there is a good deal of encyclopedic information associated with verbal signs. For example, there is nothing in the purely linguistic contrasts in the consanguineal meaning of father (one prior generation, direct line of descent, and male) to provide a basis for the use of father in speaking of God. It is only the encyclopedic information about the role of a father as protector and provider and guide (in an authoritative sense) which makes possible such a figurative extension of meaning.

In the fifth place, semiotics helps one escape from the idea that all thought and communication is restricted to the code of language. Thought may take place by means of a number of icons, for example, diagrams, mathematical formulas, picture sequences, and series of imagined episodes, and certainly religious communication frequently takes place by means of nonverbal symbols. In Christianity this is often accomplished by means of baptism, holy communion, the cross and crucifix. In some religions there is even opposition to the communication of religious faith and belief by means of words. Some Hindu gurus have even refused to talk about their religious experience, since the reality can only be experienced in transcendental ways. To attempt to translate such experience into words would be as impossible and misleading as to attempt to translate a masterpiece by Rembrandt into an oral equivalent.

CHAPTER 11

Rhetorical Features and Translation

The use of appropriate rhetorical features is crucial in translating. This is particularly true of the Bible in view of such factors as historical associations, personal preferences, and changing cultural values and attitudes. For the Holy Scriptures particularly there is a tendency to associate rhetorical forms with particular theological positions. For many people the style of the King James Version suggests orthodoxy, while the style of the New English Bible is associated with liberalism and heresy.

Distinct stylistic differences in the translation of the Bible may be viewed as serving four major purposes: acceptance, identification, impact, and esthetic appreciation. Whether a translation is acceptable to a constituency depends upon a number of factors, for example, recommendation by influential persons, promotion, availability, and price, but one long-term factor which is probably more important than anything else is style. In fact, at least in the reactions of many people, it seems even more important than accuracy. For a great many people, acceptability means that a translation should sound like a translation. Many persons are suspicious of any translation of the Bible which employs present-day language and incorporates modern rhetorical features. Perhaps it is school experience in studying a foreign language which predisposes people to think that if translations are not awkward, they cannot be faithful. Some persons, for example, insist that the New American Standard Version must be a faithful translation because it contains so many unnatural expressions. At the same time, the strangeness of "translationese" may add a touch of mystery to a text, thus suggesting some supernatural validation or reality.

Style as a factor in identification is a far more subtle feature than acceptability. People may, for example, insist on the style of the King James Version because it has been associated with early religious experience, perhaps with the form of Scripture as used by one's parents. Accordingly, its archaisms may seem to lend authority. In this connection it is interesting that so many recent sects appealing to disillusioned youth make use of the King James Version, evidently because its archaic form seems to suggest permanency and authority. For other persons, however, a translation in an obsolete style has precisely the opposite effect. Obsolete language suggests obsolete ideas, so that both the church and the Scriptures become museum pieces.

The extent to which the style of a translation carries impact depends largely upon what people are already familiar with. Anything which is too well known becomes largely redundant. Accordingly, a Bible translation in the fresh language of today suggests a content for weekdays as well as for Sunday. This, however, is precisely what some people object to, for such a style may imply a content which is too demanding. For some persons it is better to be able to admire the style while forgetting the message.

There is a universal tendency for people to want to beautify in various ways what they highly value. Therefore, many insist that any translation of the Bible must employ an elaborate, elegant style throughout, despite the considerable differences in the stylistic levels of the corresponding Hebrew and Greek texts. Such persons object to making the style of the Gospel of Mark plain and straightforward; they would much prefer to embellish the style so as to make it seem more dignified and esthetically imposing.

From the discussions in Chapters 2 and 3 of this book it should be clear that it is impossible to match various rhetorical devices from language to language by means of any automatic rules of formal correspondence. In some languages, for example, rhetorical questions are simply not employed, while in other languages rhetorical questions may be used but only when they are immediately answered in the text. In other words, the author is required to answer his question if he asks it. For many languages, however, the rhetorical equivalent of a rhetorical question is an emphatic statement. But a rhetorical question is really something more than an emphatic statement, since the question implies that the people themselves must know the answer. In fact, a rhetorical question is a way of implying an audience's agreement with the declaration. One may translate John 8.43 as "Why do you not understand what I say? It is because you cannot bear to listen to my message". An answer is given, but this combination of question and answer sounds somewhat strange and awkward. The question itself, of course, implies that the audience knows full well why they do not understand, so that one could very well reproduce the meaning of this rhetorical question and statement by a rendering such as "You know why you do not understand what I say, for you cannot bear to listen to my message".

In a number of instances it would be entirely inappropriate to represent certain stylistic features, since the features would have entirely different values in the source and receptor languages. For example, in Mark 1.16-45 the Revised Standard Version follows very closely the Greek text in rendering the Greek conjunction καί 'and'. Out of 27 sentences, 22 begin with and. Only two sentences in the RSV begin with but, one sentence begins with now, and two sentences have no conjunctive connector. Of the six paragraphs, five begin with and. This excessive use of and gives an impression of childish language. This is precisely the way many children write and speak, and it certainly does not do justice to the quite acceptable Semiticized Greek of the Gospel of Mark by trying to reproduce the numerous instances of Greek καί.

Parallelism in poetry can be fine in the use of a text for liturgical purposes, but it often seems tedious and pleonastic in a text meant for private reading. It is precisely for that reason that John Knox attempted to eliminate parallelism in his translation while compensating for its esthetic value by other rhetorical devices. For the purposes of his translation, namely private reading, he was remarkably successful.

In many instances it is inappropriate to reproduce figurative language. In Genesis 49.14, for example, Issachar is spoken of as "a strong ass", clearly, a compliment in Hebrew, but certainly not in English. To use the New Testament expression "he opened his mouth and spoke" seems in some languages to be not only awkward but absurd, for how else could a person speak without opening his mouth. In reality, this idiom simply introduces a formal utterance, and therefore the equivalent in English might very well be "he declared".

In view of the fact that one cannot match rhetorical forms, it is essential that careful consideration be given to the equivalent rhetorical functions, for these functions can in large measure be matched if one bears in mind carefully the respective degree of impact and appeal in the source and receptor texts. The question is basically "What is the function of the rhetorical feature or features?" In other words, "What is the feature or set of features a sign of?" Though the features may not be universal, the functions are, for all languages have devices for such functions as emphasis, marking similarities and contrasts, foregrounding and backgrounding, saying one thing while intending something else, and making a text more esthetically attractive.

In order to arrive at what are likely to be the rhetorical equivalents in source and receptor languages, one must first make a careful study of the rhetorical features of the source text. In the case of the study of the Bible, so much attention has been given to the theological content and to the historical processes involved in its formation, that relatively little attention has been given to matters of style. One reason for this is perhaps the fact that great attention has been focused upon the fact that the New Testament is in Koine Greek, a form of Greek rather different from the elaborate structures employed by the Atticists of Hellenistic times. Closer attention to the style of the Greek New Testament should, however, result in persons being not only more sensitive to these relevant aspects of the text but more equipped to produce equivalent expressions in translations.

In order to produce a rhetorically satisfactory translation, it is also essential to study the rhetorical features of the receptor language. Unfortunately, within the last generation or so, interest in technology and a desire for uninhibited self-expression seem to have conspired to almost eliminate interest in rhetoric. School systems often seem satisfied if they can induce students to avoid some of the more gross errors in composition, and school systems often seem content if students can write at least intelligible, if not elegant, English.

On the basis of a more satisfactory and comprehensive understanding of the functions of rhetorical features in both the source and receptor language, it is usually possible to set up a series of rhetorical equivalents, but one cannot apply such a set without careful consideration of the particular context and the audience for which a translation is being prepared. People's preconceptions as to what makes a translation effective and acceptable are a major consideration.

There are, however, significant limits as to the number and type of adjustments which can be made in rhetorical features. In the interest of rhetorical similarities between languages, one must not violate the integrity of the source text itself. For example, one translator argued that in a particular language the story of the Prodigal Son should be recast in quite a different form, since in the language in question such stories normally began at a crucial point and then used backflashes to fill out the historical setting. Accordingly, this translator wished to begin the story of the prodigal son with the younger son in the pigpen, forced by famine to eat what the pigs were eating. This may sound rhetorically appropriate in some receptor language, but as already noted, this parable in Luke 15 is not really the story of the prodigal son but the story of the relationship between a father and two sons, in other words a family triad corresponding to the triad in the communicative setting.

One of the serious problems involved in attempting to find rhetorical equivalents between source and receptor languages is the fact that so many of the rhetorical features, particularly various types of figurative usage, are cultural specialities, that is to say, they depend so largely upon the cultural context to provide meaning. Therefore, in translation there is a tendency to substitute for such figurative expressions nonfigurative parallels. The result of this process, however, involves almost inevitably a loss in impact. As a result, one must calculate not only how best to render a particular rhetorical feature, but how to compensate for the loss of impact by incorporating into the text rhetorical features of the receptor language which may not specifically represent corresponding features in the source text. In other words, if a number of figurative expressions in the source text must be rendered by means of nonfigurative language in order to make them intelligible, it is essential that some of the loss of impact be compensated for by rendering a number of nonfigurative expressions in the source text by means of figurative words and phrases in the receptor text. Only in this way can one ultimately

obtain an equivalent degree of impact. In the process of
introducing compensatory features, it is, of course, essential to avoid those which would be anachronistic, prejudi-
cial to the content, or not in keeping with the level of
language. One way to avoid serious mistakes is to carefully
evaluate the semiotic effect of the corresponding rhetorical
features.

APPENDIX

TOWARD A NEW CLASSIFICATION OF THE FIGURES (σχήματα) IN THE
GREEK NEW TESTAMENT 1

A cursory view of the classification of the figures by some
prominent grammarians of New Testament Greek reveals a quite
confusing picture. In his monumental work A Grammar of the
Greek New Testament in the Light of Historical Research
(1919), A.T. Robertson deals with certain "grammatical"
figures of speech in his discussion of the sentence (chapter
10, 390-445). The "remaining" figures are dealt with in
chapter 22 under the heading: Figures of Speech (1194-
1208), and they are divided into figures of idea or thought
(σχήματα διανοίας, 1198-1199) and figures of expression
(σχήματα λέξεως, 1199-1208).

Blass-Debrunner-Rehkopf has similar distinctions. The last
four chapters (12-15) of Grammatik des neutestamentlichen
Griechisch (1979) are devoted to the topic of style. Chapter 12 (Satzfügung) contains such figures as asyndeton,
parenthesis and anacoluthon, while chapter 13 (Wort und
Satzstellung) deals with the position of words and phrases
in a sentence, and includes figures like hyperbaton, chiasm
etc. (parr. 472-478). Chapter 14 is devoted to the figures
of ellipse, brachylogy and pleonasm (parr. 479-484). After
thus dealing with typical figures of speech in chapters
12-14, the last chapter has as its heading: Komposition der
Worte: Figuren (parr. 485-496). The figures are divided
into σχήματα λέξεως (Figuren des Ausdrucks, parr. 486-494)
and σχήματα διανοίας (Figuren des Gedankens, parr. 495-
496).

---

1   This classification was prepared in cooperation with
     dr. E. A. Nida, and prof. J. P. Louw at a seminar in
     Bloemfontein, January 1982.

It is clear that the main division lies between the grammatical and syntactical figures on the one hand, and the rhetorical figures on the other. The rhetorical figures are divided into figures of expression and figures of thought. These distinctions cause certain problems.

To begin with, it is doubtful whether the grammatical/syntactical and the rhetorical figures can be separated from one another as unequivocally as most grammarians do. The basis or principle for such a distinction is not at all evident, because most of the so-called rhetorical figures are based on an unusual grammatical or syntactical arrangement. (Symploke, for instance, has to do with an unusual syntactical arrangement, treated by Blass-Debrunner-Rehkopf as one of the σχήματα λέξεως in par. 491, i.e. as one of the rhetorical figures.) This fact accounts for the unsatisfactory treatment of typical figures of speech under such headings as Sentence (Robertson) and Satzfügung (Blass-Debrunner-Rehkopf).

Furthermore, the distinction between the figures of expression and the figures of thought is also disputable. It first occurs in the Rhetorica ad Herennium, a hellenistic work from the first century B.C. According to H. Caplan, Ad Herennium (Loeb, 1977, 275) the line of demarcation between the figures of thought and the figures of diction was a vague one even in Hellenistic times. Nevertheless, both Cicero and Quintillian use the distinction in their theoretical works. Despite its vagueness, it also forms the basis for the classification of the figures (next to the tropes) in the works of R. Volkmann, Die Rhetorik der Griechen und Römer (1963), H. Lausberg, Elemente der literarischen Rhetorik (1963) and J. Martin, Antike Rhetorik (1974).

The distinction between the σχήματα λέξεως and σχήματα διανοίας is a classical distinction and suits the classical authors, whose rhetorical system distinguished between the so-called πραγματικὸς τόπος and λεκτικὸς τόπος. These classical rhetorical categories, however, do not form the general basis of the presentation of material in the New Testament. Is it therefore a useful distinction for the classification of the figures in the Greek New Testament?

Lastly, apart from the distinction between the σχήματα λέξεως and σχήματα διανοίας, most grammars have no further distinctions. The result is that the figures are simply listed without any diagnostic principle for classification. And when an attempt is made at a further classification of the figures, the principles of classification become obscure. Blass-Debrunner-Rehkopf, for example, classifies asyndeton and elleipsis under two headings, namely Satzfügung (parr. 459-463) and then a separate chapter devoted to Ellipse, Brachylogie, Pleonasmus (parr. 479-484). The principle underlying both asyndeton and elleipsis, however, is the same, namely omission, while the reason for grouping only elleipsis, brachylogy and pleonasm together is not quite clear.

In what follows an attempt is made to classify all the figures according to three basic principles: repetition, omission and shift in expectancies. Each principle has various sub-divisions (see below), and each division is provided with an example from the Greek New Testament. Some technical terms are put between brackets for the initiated reader, while an attempt is made to arrange the categories in such a way that they are self-evident without any further comment. (See also the synopsis on pages 188-190.)

I   REPETITION

    A   Repetition of the same forms and the same meanings

1 <u>With single items</u>

a) Contiguous (Anadiplosis)

σταύρου, σταύρου αὐτόν

(Crucify, crucify him) (Lk 23:21).

See also Lk 10:41, Lk 6:46, Mk 6:39.

b) Non-contiguous

(i) Structurally significant positions

i Reference to the non-linguistic

world

- Initial position (Epanaphora)

πάντα στέγει, πάντα πιστεύει, πάντα

ἐλπίζει, πάντα ὑπομένει.

(It bears all things, believes all

things, hopes all things, endures

all things) (1 Cor 13:7)

- Final position (Epiphora)

οὐ γὰρ δήπου ἀγγέλων ἐπιλαμβάνεται,

ἀλλὰ σπέρματος Ἀβραὰμ ἐπιλαμβάνεται

(For clearly he does not help the

angels, but he helps the descen-

dants of Abraham) (He 2:16)

See also 1 Cor 7:27, 1 Cor 13:11.

- Initial and final positions in sub-

sequent clauses (Symploke)

οὐ δύνασθε ποτήριον κυρίου πίνειν

καὶ ποτήριον δαιμονίων· οὐ δύνασθε

τραπέζης κυρίου μετέχειν καὶ τρα-

πέζης δαιμονίων (You cannot drink

the cup of the Lord, and the cup of

demons; you cannot be partakers of

the Lord's table, and of the table

of demons. (1 Cor 10:21).

- The sequence AB, BC, CD, DE etc.
  (Climax)

  οὐ μόνον δέ, ἀλλὰ καὶ καυχώμεθα ἐν
  ταῖς <u>θλίψεσιν</u>, εἰδότες ὅτι ἡ <u>θλῖψις</u>
  ὑπομονὴν κατεργάζεται, ἡ δὲ ὑπομονὴ
  δοκιμήν, ἡ δὲ δοκιμὴ ἐλπίδα· ἡ δὲ
  ἐλπὶς οὐ καταισχύνει.....

  (Not only so, but we also boast of
  our troubles, knowing that trouble
  produces endurance, endurance produces approval, and approval produces hope, and hope does not disappoint) (Rm 5:3-5)
  See also Rm 8:30.

- Final position in previous clause
  and initial position in the next
  clause (Anastrophe)

  μὴ ζήτει <u>λύσιν·</u> <u>λέλυσαι</u> ἀπὸ
  γυναικός;

  (Seek not to be loosed; are you
  loosed from a wife?) (1 Cor 7:27)

- Initial position in the previous
  clause and final position in the
  next clause (Kyklos)

  τῇ γὰρ <u>ἐλπίδι</u>, ἐσώθημεν· ἐλπὶς δὲ
  βλεπομένη οὐκ ἔστιν <u>ἐλπίς</u>.

  (For we are saved by hope; but hope
  that is seen is not hope) (Rm 8:24)

ii Reference to the linguistic world

- Identical bound forms with the same
  meaning in analogous positions
  (Homoeoteleuton, Alliteration)

καταλάλ<u>ους</u>, θεοστυγεῖς, ὑβριστ<u>άς</u>,
ὑπερηφάν<u>ους</u>, ἀλαζόν<u>ας</u>, ἐφευρετ<u>άς</u>
κακῶν, γονεῦσιν ἀπειθεῖς, ἀσυνέ-
τ<u>ους</u>, ἀσυνθέτ<u>ους</u>, ἀστόργ<u>ους</u>,
ἀνελεήμον<u>ας</u>

(Backbiters, haters of God, de-
spiteful, proud, boasters, inven-
tors of evil things, disobedient to
parents, without understanding,
disloyal, without natural affec-
tion, unmerciful) (Rm 1:30-31)
See also Rm 12:15.

(ii) Non-structurally significant position
    i Referring to the non-linguistic world
      (Anaphora)
      σῶμα (body) in the pericope 1 Cor 12:
      12-26.
      See also ἀνάστασις (resurrection),
      ἐγήγερται (be risen) etc. in 1 Cor
      15:12-58.

    ii Referring to the linguistic world
      (Polysundeton)
      παραδοθήσεται γὰρ τοῖς ἔθνεσιν <u>καὶ</u>
      ἐμπαιχθήσεται <u>καὶ</u> ὑβρισθήσεται
      <u>καὶ</u> ἐμπτυσθήσεται, <u>καὶ</u> μαστιγώσαντες
      ἀποκτενοῦσιν αὐτόν
      (For he shall be delivered unto the
      Gentiles, and shall be mocked, and
      spitefully entreated, and spitted on:
      and they shall scourge him and put
      him to death). (Lk 18:32-33).
      See also the use of καί in Mark.

2.   <u>With two or more items</u>
    a) Structurally significant position in the
      same text

(i) Same lexical units

    i Parallel (Anaphora)

    ἐὰν εἴπωμεν (if we say) in 1 Jn 1:
6-10.

    See also ἐρρέθη (τοῖς ἀρχαίοις) (it
was said by them of old time) in Mt
5:21-43.

    ii Inverted parallelism (Chiasm)

$$A \quad\quad B \quad\quad\quad\quad C$$
τὸ σάββατον διὰ τὸν ἄνθρωπον ἐγένετο
$$C \quad\quad\quad\quad B \quad\quad A$$
καὶ οὐχ ὁ ἄνθρωπος διὰ τὸ σάββατον
(The sabbath was made for man, and not
man for the sabbath.) (Mk 2:27)

$$A \quad B$$
See also Jn 1:1....καὶ ὁ λόγος ἦν πρὸς
$$C \quad\quad\quad C \quad B \quad\quad A$$
τὸν θεόν, καὶ θεὸς ἦν ὁ λόγος.
(...and the Word was with God, and the
Word was God)

    iii Mixed [2)]

$$A \quad\quad B \quad\quad C \quad\quad\quad D$$
ὑμεῖς ἐστε τὸ ἅλας τῆς γῆς....
$$A \quad\quad B \quad\quad E \quad\quad\quad F$$
ὑμεῖς ἐστε τὸ φῶς τοῦ κόσμου
(You are the salt of the earth; You
are the light of the world) (Mt 5:13-
14). See also Jn 5:30.

(ii) Different lexical units

    i Parallel (Semantic parallelism, Sunonu-
mia)

$$A \quad\quad B \quad\quad\quad\quad C$$
μεγαλύνει ἡ ψυχή μου τὸν κύριον,

A   B

καὶ ἠγαλλίασεν τὸ πνεῦμα μου ἐπὶ τῷ

C

θεῷ

(My soul magnifies the Lord, and my
spirit rejoiced in God) (Lk 1:47)
See also 1 Cor 10:21 quoted above.

    ii Inverted (Semantic chiasm)

ὅτι τὸν ἥλιον αὐτοῦ ἀνατέλλει ἐπὶ

A   B

πονηροὺς καὶ ἀγαθοὺς καὶ βρέχει ἐπὶ

B   A

δικαίους καὶ ἀδίκους.

(For he makes his sun to rise on the
evil and on the good, and sends rain on
the just and on the unjust) (Mt 5:45)

    iii Mixed
    No examples.

  b) Structurally significant position in diffe-
     rent texts (Emphasis)
     ἐν ἀρχῇ ἦν ὁ λόγος...
     (In the beginning was the Word) (Jn 1:1, if
     it refers to Gen 1:1)

B   Similar or identical forms with different meanings

  1 Similar forms with different meanings (Parono-
    masia)
    λιμοὶ καὶ λοιμοὶ ἔσονται
    (There shall be famines and pestilences) (Lk
    21:11)
    See also   Acts 8:30 with γινώσκεις...ἀναγινώσ-
    κεις.

        (Understand you what you read?)

Rm 1:29 with φθόνου, φόνου
(envy murder)

2 Identical forms with different meanings (Dia-
phora)
πνεῦμα (spirit, wind) in Jn 3:6-8.
See also ἦν (to exist, to be in a place, to
have the nature of) in Jn 1:1.

3 Same length in successive clauses, with different meanings (Isocolon)
οὐ χαίρει ἐπὶ τῇ ἀδικίᾳ,
συγχαίρει δὲ τῇ ἀληθείᾳ.
(It is not happy with iniquity,
but it is happy with the truth) (1 Cor 13:6)
See also 1 Cor 13:7.

4 Same sentence structure in successive
clauses, with different meanings (Parison)

    1   2   3   4
ὥσπερ γὰρ διὰ τῆς παρακοῆς τοῦ ἑνὸς ἀνθρώπου
  5   6   7
ἁμαρτωλοὶ κατεστάθησαν οἱ πολλοί,

  1   2   3   4   5
οὕτως καὶ διὰ τῆς ὑπακοῆς τοῦ ἑνὸς δίκαιοι
  6   7
κατασταθήσονται οἱ πολλοί
(For as by one man's disobedience many were
made sinners, so by the obedience of one
shall many be made righteous) (Rm 5:19).

5 Same length and sentence structure in successive clauses, with different meanings (Parho-
moiosis)

　　　　1 ′2　　　3　　　　4
　　ὑμεῖς ἐστε τὸ ἅλας τῆς γῆς.....
　　　　1　2　　　3　　　　4
　　ὑμεῖς ἐστε τὸ φῶς τοῦ κόσμου
　　(You are the salt of the earth;
　　You are the light of the world) (Mt 5:13-14)

C　Different forms with the same meaning (Pleo-
　nasm)
　καὶ πάλιν ὑπέστρεψα εἰς Δαμασκόν
　(And I returned again unto Damascus) (Gal
　1:17)
　See also x πάλιν ἀνακάμψω
　　　　　　　　(I will return again) (Acts
　　　　　　　　18:21).
　　　　　x ἀλήθειαν λέγω...οὐ ψεύδομαι
　　　　　　　　(I tell the truth...I do not lie)
　　　　　　　　(Rm 9:1).
　　　　　x φῶς ἐστιν...σκοτία...οὐκ ἔστιν
　　　　　　　　οὐδεμία
　　　　　　　　(He is Light and no darkness is
　　　　　　　　in him) (1 Jn 1:5)
　　　　　x ἀποκριθεὶς αὐτοῖς λέγει
　　　　　　　　(Answering them, he said) (Mt
　　　　　　　　4.4).

D　Different forms with opposite meanings (Anti-
　thesis)
　οὔτε ὕψωμα οὔτε βάθος οὔτε τις κτίσις
　ἑτέρα...
　(Nor height, nor depth, nor any other crea-
　ture.) (Rm 8:39).
　See also 1 Cor 1:27 fol., 1 Cor 15,42 fol.

II OMISSION

A　Words important for the referential context

1   <u>Analogous position</u>

    a) The same word (Zeugma)
    καὶ προσελθὼν ὁ τὰ πέντε τάλαντα
    <u>λαβὼν</u> προσήνεγκεν ἄλλα πέντε τάλαντα
    λέγων...προσελθὼν δὲ καὶ ὁ τὰ δύο
    τάλαντα <u>(λαβὼν)</u> εἶπεν...
    (And so he that had received five talents
    came and brought other five talents, say-
    ing...He also (that had received) two ta-
    lents came and said...) (Mt 25:20-22).

    b) Different words (Sullepsis)
    γάλα ὑμᾶς <u>ἐπότισα</u>, οὐ βρῶμα <u>(ἐψώμισα)</u>
    (I gave you milk to drink, not meat (to
    eat)) (1 Cor 3:2).

    c) Purposeful omission of consequence (Apo-
    siopesis)
    ἀλλ' <u>εἴ τι δύνῃ</u>, βοήθησον ἡμῖν σπλα-
    γχνισθεὶς ἐφ' ἡμᾶς. ὁ δὲ Ἰησοῦς εἶπεν
    αὐτῷ, Τὸ Εἰ δύνῃ - πάντα δυνατὰ τῷ
    πιστεύοντι.
    (But if you can do anything, have compas-
    sion on us and help us. Jesus said unto
    him: If you can - all things are possible
    for the person who has faith) (Mk 9:22-23)

2   <u>Non-analogous position</u> (Brachylogia)
    εἶπαν οὖν αὐτῷ, Τίς εἶ; ἵνα ἀπόκρισιν δῶμεν
    τοῖς πέμψασιν ἡμᾶς. τί λέγεις περὶ σεαυτοῦ;
    (Then they said unto him: Who are you? that
    we may give answer to them that sent us. What
    do you say about yourself?) (Jn 1:22).

B   <u>Words important for the linguistic context</u>
   (Elleipsis and asyndeton)

οὐ γὰρ ὁ ἐν τῷ φανερῷ Ἰουδαῖός ἐστιν, οὐδὲ ἡ
ἐν τῷ φανερῷ ἐν σαρκὶ περιτομή (ἐστιν)·
ἀλλ᾽ ὁ ἐν τῷ κρυπτῷ Ἰουδαῖος (ἐστιν),
καὶ περιτομὴ καρδίας ἐν πνεύματι οὐ
γράμματι (ἐστιν)...
(For he is not a Jew, who is one outwardly; neither (is) that circumcision, which (is) outward in
the flesh; but he (is) a Jew, who is one inward-
ly; and circumcision (is) that of the heart, in
the spirit...) (Rm 2:28-29).
(Elleipsis)

For asyndeton, see Mk 2:11, 1 Cor 13:13.

C Deep-structure omissions

- Taboo forms
   μακάριοι οἱ πενθοῦντες,
   ὅτι αὐτοὶ παρακληθήσονται
   (Blessed are they that mourn, for God will
   comfort them.) (Mt 5:4).
   See also the remaining beatitudes.

III FORMS INVOLVING A SHIFT IN EXPECTANCIES

A Shifts in expectancies of the word-order

   1 Unusual position in a clause (Hyperbaton)
      Ἰάκωβος θεοῦ καὶ κυρίου Ἰησοῦ Χριστοῦ
      δοῦλος...
      (James, a servant of God and of the Lord Je-
      sus Christ...) (James 1:1).
      See also James 1:7-8.

   2 Unusual position outside the clause (Prolep-
      sis)

καὶ περὶ ἐνδύματος τί μεριμνᾶτε; καταμάθετε
<u>τὰ κρίνα τοῦ ἀγροῦ</u> πῶς αὐξάνουσιν.
(And why worry about clothes? Look how the
flowers of the field grow.) (Mt 6:28).
See also Rm 9:19-20.

3   <u>Insertion</u> (Parenthesis, Dihorthosis)
πολλάκις προεθέμην ἐλθεῖν πρὸς ὑμᾶς,
<u>καὶ ἐκωλύθην ἄχρι τοῦ δεῦρο</u>, ἵνα τινὰ
καρπὸν σχῶ...
(Many times I have planned to visit you - but
I have been prevented up to the present - in
order that I might have some results among
you) (Rm 1:13) (Parenthesis)
See also 2 Cor 11:21, Rev 3:8.

B   <u>Shifts in expectancies of the syntax</u> (Anacoluthon,
synekdoche)
<u>ὁ γὰρ Μωϋσῆς οὗτος</u>, ὃς ἐξήγαγεν ἡμᾶς ἐκ γῆς
Αἰγύπτου, οὐκ οἴδαμεν τί ἐγένετο <u>αὐτῷ</u>
(For that man Moses, who brought us out of Egypt,
we do not know what has happened to him) (Acts
7:40) (Anacoluthon).
See also Acts 1:4, Rm 1:6-8.

For synekdoche (plural for singular), see Rm
1:1+5:
<u>Παῦλος δοῦλος</u> Χριστοῦ Ἰησοῦ...δι' οὗ <u>ἐλάβομεν</u>
<u>χάριν</u>...
(Paul, a servant of Christ Jesus...by whom we have
received grace...)

C   <u>Shifts in propositions</u>
1   <u>Apparent contradictions</u> (Oxymoron, Paradoxon)
καὶ γὰρ <u>οὐ δεδόξασται</u> <u>τὸ δεδοξασμένον</u>...ἐν
τούτῳ τῷ μέρει εἵνεκεν τῆς ὑπερβαλλούσης
δόξης

(For that which has been made glorious has
not been made glorious....) (2 Cor 3:10)
(Oxymoron).

See also 2 Tim 2:12 with ἀπιστοῦμεν, ἐκεῖνος
πιστὸς μένει (if we are not faithful, he
remains faithful)

For a Paradoxon, see 1 Cor 1:27-28.

2   Contradiction in content and intent

a)   Saying exactly the opposite of what you
     intend to say (Eironeia)
     χαρίσασθέ μοι τὴν ἀδικίαν ταύτην
     (For how is it that you were treated
     worse than the other churches, except
     for the fact that I myself was no bur-
     den to you? Forgive me for this in-
     justice) (2 Cor 12:13).

b)   The deliberate use of understatement to
     increase the effect of what is intended
     (Litotes)
     ὅτι οὐκ ἀδυνήσει παρὰ τοῦ θεοῦ πᾶν ῥῆμα
     (Because with God anything is not impos-
     sible) (Lk 1:37).
     See also Rm 1:16, 10:16.

c)   Exaggeration (Hyperbole)
     ἔσχατον δὲ πάντων ὡσπερεὶ τῷ ἐκτρώματι
     ὤφθη κἀμοί
     (And the entire city was gathered at the
     door) (Mk 1:33).
     See also 2 Cor 11:8, with ἄλλας ἐκκλη-
     σίας ἐσύλησα (I robbed other churches).

d) To proceed, contrary to statement (Paraleipsis)

περὶ δὲ τῶν χρόνων καὶ τῶν καιρῶν, ἀδελφοί, <u>οὐ χρείαν ἔχετε ὑμῖν γράφεσθαι</u>...

(But about the times and occasions, brothers, there is no need to write to you. For you yourselves know very well that...) (1 Thes 5:1-2).

See also 2 Cor 9:1.

D   Shifts with regard to the communication function

1   The rhetorical question (Erotema)

εἰ ὁ θεὸς ὑπὲρ ἡμῶν, τίς καθ᾽ ἡμῶν;

(If God is for us, who can be against us?) (Rm 8:31).

See also Gal 2:14.

2   Question and answer (Dialektikon)[3]

τί οὖν ἐροῦμεν; ἐπιμένωμεν τῇ ἁμαρτίᾳ, ἵνα ἡ χάρις πλεονάσῃ; μὴ γένοιτο.

(What shall we say then? Shall we continue in sin, that grace may abound? God forbid!) (Rm 6:1-2).

See also Rm 6:15, 7:7,13.

3   Literal and figurative meaning (Metaphora, Metonumia, Prosopopoiia)

ὁ λόγος τοῦ θεοῦ ηὔξανεν

(And the word of God increased) (Acts 6:7) (Metaphora).

See also Rm 11:18, James 1:15, Jn 15:1 fol. Lk 1:66 etc.

Under this category we can also include
idioms, the meaning of parables, allegories (in terms of Peirce's thirdness
level) etc. The New Testament abounds
in idioms[4], for example:

ἀναζωσάμενοι τὰς ὀσφύας τῆς διανοίας
ὑμῶν

(girding up the loins of your mind)
(1 Pet 1:13).
See also Mt 6:2, Rm 12:20, 2 Cor 12:9.

E <u>Shifts between meaning and referent</u> (Periphrasis,
Antonomasia)
οἶδα ἄνθρωπον ἐν Χριστῷ πρὸ ἐτῶν δεκατεσσάρων...
ἁρπαγέντα τὸν τοιοῦτον <u>ἕως τρίτου οὐρανοῦ</u>
(I knew a man in Christ above fourteen years ago..
that such a man was caught up to the third heaven)
(= the place where God is) (2 Cor 12:2) (Periphrasis).

IV <u>MEASUREMENT OF UNITS</u>[5]
(Gnome, aphorism)
καὶ εἴρηκέν μοι, Ἀρκεῖ σοι ἡ χάρις μου· <u>ἡ γὰρ δύναμις</u>
<u>ἐν ἀσθενείᾳ τελεῖται</u>
(See also Rm.12:20)

To conclude: Obviously there is much more to style than the
figures of speech discussed above, e.g. the selection and
ordering of content, the genre etc. And concerning the figures themselves, it is impossible to enumerate all the
examples of each category distinguished in the preceding
paragraphs, or to discuss their various functions. The sole
aim of this article is to provide a framework for a more
basic approach towards the classification of figures in the
Greek New Testament, taking into account the distinctive
character of the New Testament and providing a practical
instrument for recognizing the numerous figures one may
encounter in the Greek of the New Testament.

SINOPSIS

I REPETITION

   A <u>Repetition of same forms and same meanings</u>

       1 <u>With single items</u>

          a) Contiguous (Anadiplosis)

          b) Non-contiguous

              (i) In structurally significant positions

                  i Reference to the non-linguistic world

                    - Initial position (Epanaphora)

                    - Final position (Epiphora)

                    - Initial and final positions in subsequent clauses (Symploke)

                    - The sequence AB, BC, CD, etc. (Climax)

                    - Final position in previous and initial position in the next clause (Anastrophe)

                    - Initial position in the previous and final position in the next clause (Kyklos)

                  ii Reference to the linguistic world

                    - Identical bound forms with the same meaning in analogous positions (Homoeoteleuton, Alliteration)

              (ii) Non-structurally significant position

                  i Referring to the non-linguistic world (Anaphora)

                  ii Referring to the linguistic world (Polysyndeton)

       2. <u>With two or more items</u>

          a) Structurally significant position in the same text

        (i) Same lexical units

            i   Parallel (Anaphora)

           ii   Inverted parallelism (Chiasm)

         iii   Mixed

       (ii) Different lexical units

            i   Parallel (Semantic parallel-
ism, Sunonumia)

           ii   Inverted (Semantic chiasm)

         iii   Mixed

    b) Structurally significant position in different texts (Emphasis)

B.   <u>Similar or identical forms with different meanings</u>

    1.   <u>Similar forms with different meanings</u> (Paro-
nomasia)

    2.   <u>Identical forms with different meanings</u> (Dia-
phora)

    3.   <u>Same length in successive clauses, with dif-
ferent meanings</u> (Isocolon)

    4.   <u>Same structure in successive clauses, with
different meanings</u> (Parison)

    5.   <u>Same length and structure in successive
clauses, with different meanings</u> (Parho-
moiosis)

C.   <u>Different forms with the same meaning</u> (Pleonasm)

D.   <u>Different forms with opposite meanings</u> (Anti-
thesis)

II   OMISSION

    A   <u>Words important for the referential context</u>

       1.   <u>Analogous position</u>

          a)   The same word (Zeugma)

          b)   Different words (Sullepsis)

          c)   Purposeful omission of consequence
(Aposiopesis)

2.   Non-analogous position (Brachylogia)

B   Words important for the linguistic context (Ellipsis and asyndeton)

C   Deep-structure omissions
     Taboo forms

III   FORMS INVOLVING A SHIFT IN EXPECTANCIES
A   Shifts in expectancies of the word-order
1.   Unusual position in a clause (Hyperbaton)
2.   Unusual position outside the clause (Prolepsis)
3.   Insertion (Parenthesis, Dihorthosis)

B   Shifts in expectancies of the syntax (Anacoluthon; synekdoche)

C   Shifts in propositions
1.   Apparent contradictions (Oxymoron, Paradoxon)
2.   Contradiction in content and intent
     a)   Saying exactly the opposite of what you intend to say (Eironeia)
     b)   The deliberate use of understatement to increase the effect of what is intended (Litotes)
     c)   Exaggeration (Hyperbole)
     d)   To proceed, contrary to statement (Paraleipsis)

D   Shifts with regard to the communication function
1.   The rhetorical question (Erotema)
2.   Question and answer (Dialektikon)
3.   Literal and figurative meaning (Metaphora, Metonumia, Prosopopoiia)
     -    Idioms, parables, allegories

E   Shifts between meaning and referent (Periphrasis, Antonomasia)

IV   MEASUREMENT OF UNITS (Gnome, aphorism)...

FOOTNOTES

2) Mixed, that is, only certain lexical units correspond while the syntactic structure of both phrases is thé same.

3) The shift consists in the question being answered by the same person.

4) Idioms or *gnomai* are expressions consisting of two or more words, whose meaning is not to be derived from the sum total of the parts.

5) This principle applies mainly to poetry, where the limitation on the length of lines is an important factor. Certain figures of speech, however, are also concerned with matters of relative length, e.g. proverbs, riddles and aphorisms. Brevity here is not obtained by omitting certain lexical units, but by conveying the maximum information by means of the minimum amount of lexical units.

A.H. SNYMAN

J.v.W. CRONJé

BIBLIOGRAPHY

Allerton, D.J. 1979 Essentials of Grammatical Theory: A
    Consensus View of Syntax and Morphology London:
    Routledge and Paul

Alter, Robert 1981 The Art of Biblical Narrative New York:
    Basic Books, Inc

Anderson, John M. 1971 The Grammar of Case Cambridge: at
    the University Press

Apresjan, Ju. D. 1971 Ideen und Methoden der modernen struk-
    turellen Linguistik Berlin: Akademie-Verlag

Austin, John L. 1962 How to Do Things with Words Cambridge,
    Mass.: Harvard University Press

Baron, Naomi S. 1979 Linguistics and Semiotics: two dis-
    ciplines in search of a subject Semiotica 26.289-310

Beaugrande, Robert de and Wolfgang U. Dressler 1981 Intro-
    duction to Text Linguistics London and New York:
    Longman

Bierwisch, Manfred 1969 On certain problems of semantic re-
    presentations Foundations of Language 5.153-184

    1971 Structuralism: history, problems, and methods. In
    Jens Ihwe ed. Literaturwissenschaft und Linguistik
    Frankfurt-am-Main: Athenäum Verlag

Black, Mathew 1954 An Aramaic Approach to the Gospels and
    Acts Oxford: Oxford University Press

Bolinger, Dwight 1966 Transformulation: structural transla-
    tion Acta Linguistica Hafniensa 9.130-144

Chafe, Wallace L. 1970 Meaning and the Structure of Language
    Chicago: University of Chicago Press

Chomsky, Noam 1965 Aspects of the Theory of Syntax Cambrid-
    ge, Mass.: M.I.T. Press

    1972 Studies on Semantics in Generative Grammar The
    Hague: Mouton

Coseriu, Eugenio 1970 Semantik, innere Sprachform und
    Tiefenstruktur Folia Linguistica 4.53-63

Culler, Jonathan 1975 Structuralist Poetics: Structuralism,
    Linguistics and the Study of Literature Ithaca, New
    York: Cornell University Press

Derrida, Jacques 1967 L´écriture et la différence Paris: Seuil

Dijk, Teun A. van 1975 Formal semantics of metaphorical discourse Poetics 4.173-198

Dressler, Wolfgang U. 1972 Einführung in die Textlinguistik Tübingen: Max Niemeyer Verlag

Drijepondt, H.L.F. 1979 Die antike Theorie der Varietas Spudasmata Hildesheim: Georg Olms Verlag

Eco, Umberto 1979 A Theory of Semiotics Bloomington, Indiana: Indiana University Press

Fillmore, C.J. 1967 The case of case In E. Bach and R. Harms (eds.) Proceedings of the 1967 Texas Conference on Language Universals, pp. 1-88 New York: Holt, Rinehart and Winston

Fowler, Roger 1977 Linguistics and the Novel London & New York: Methuen

Friedrich, Paul 1979 Language, Context, and the Imagination Stanford, Calif.: Stanford University Press

Goodenough, Ward H. 1956 Componential analysis and the study of meaning Language 32.195-216

Greimas, A.J. 1966 Sémantique structurale Paris: Larousse

Grimes, Joseph E. 1972 The Thread of Discourse Ithaca, New York: Department of Modern Languages and Linguistics, Cornell University

Halliday, M.A.K. 1970 Descriptive linguistics in literary studies. In Donald C. Freeman, ed. Linguistics and Literary Style, pp. 57-72 New York: Holt, Rinehart and Winston, Inc.

1975 Learning How to Mean: Explorations in the Development of Language London: Edward Arnold

Harris, Zellig S. 1951 Methods in Structural Linguistics Chicago: University of Chicago Press

Holyoak, Keith J. 1982 An analogical framework for literary interpretation Poetics 11.105-126

Honeck, Richard P., Judith Sugar, and Clare T. Kibler 1982 Stories, categories and figurative meaning Poetics 11.127-144

Hymes, Dell 1974 Foundations in Sociolinguistics: An Ethnographic Approach Philadelphia: University of Pennsylvania Press

Jakobson, Roman 1960 Linguistics and poetics In Thomas A. Sebeok, ed. Style in Language, pp. 350-377 Cambridge, Mass.: Technology Press

1970 Main Trends in the Science of Language New York: Harper & Row

1972 Verbal communication Scientific American 227 (September) 72-81

Joos, Martin 1958 Semology: a linguistic theory of meaning Studies in Linguistics 13.53-70

1962 The five clocks International Journal of American Linguistics 28, No. 2, Part 5

Katz, Jerrold J. 1972 Semantic Theory New York: Harper and Row

Kennedy, G. 1963 The Art of Persuasion in Greece Princeton: Princeton University Press

1972 The Art of Rhetoric in the Roman World Princeton: Princeton University Press

Krampen, Martin 1979 Profusion of signs without confusion Ars Semeiotica 2.327-359

Leech, Geoffrey N. and Michael H. Short 1981 Style in Fiction London and New York: Longman

Lehrer, Adrienne 1974 Semantic Fields and Lexical Structure Amsterdam, London: North-Holland Publishing Company

Levin, Samuel R. 1978 On meaning and truth in the interpretation of poetry Poetics 7.339-350

Léni-Strauss, Claude 1951 Language and the analysis of social laws American Anthropologist 53.155-163

Louw, P.J. 1973 Discourse Analysis and the Greek New Testament The Bible Translator 24, 1.101-118

1975 Semantiek en Antieke Retoriek Acta Classica 18.99-108

1982 Semantics of New Testament Greek Philadelphia: Fortress Press

1982 Veranderde Taalinsigte Johannesburg, South Africa: Randse Afrikaanse Universiteit

Ludskanov, Alexander 1975 A semiotic approach to the theory of translation Language Sciences 33.5-8

Lyons, John 1968 Introduction to Theoretical Linguistics Cambridge, Mass.: Cambridge University Press

Ludskanov, Alexander 1975 A semiotic approach to the theory of translation Language Sciences 33.5-8

Lyons, John 1968 Intoroduction to Theoretical Linguistics Cambridge, Mass.: Cambridge University Press

McClawley, James D. 1968 Concerning the base component of a transformational grammar Foundations of Language 4.243-269

Merrell, Floyd 1979 Some signs that preceded their times: or, Are we really ready for Peirce? Ars Semeiotica 2.149-172

Morris, Charles 1964 Signification and Significance Cambridge, Mass.: M.I.T. Press

Nida, Eugene A. 1964 Toward a Science of Translating Leiden: E.J. Brill

1975 Componential Analysis of Meaning The Hague: Mouton

1975 Exploring Semantic Structures München: Wilhelm Fink Verlag

1975 Language Structure and Translation: Essays by Eugene A. Nida (Selected and introduced by Anwar S. Dil) Stanford, Calif.: Stanford University Press

1982 Signs, Sense, and Translation Pretoria, South Africa: Pretoria University

and Charles R. Taber 1974 The Theory and Practice of Translation Leiden: E.J. Brill

Nilsen, Don Lee Fred 1972 Toward a Semantic Specification of Deep Case The Hague: Mouton

Patte Daniel 1980 One text: several structures Semeia 18.3.22

Peirce, Charles 1934 Collected Papers Cambridge: Harvard University Press

Petofi, Janos S. 1972 Zu einer grammatischen Theorie sprachlicher Texte Zeitschrift für Literaturwissenschaft und Linguistik 5.31-58

Ryan, Marie-Laure 1981 On the why, what and how of generic taxonomy Poetics 10.109-126

Sapir, Edward 1930 Totality Language Monograph No. 6, Baltimore: Waverly Press

1944 Grading, a study in semantics Philosophy of Science 11.93-116

Schmidt, S.H.J. ed. 1970 Text, Bedeutung, Ästhetik München: Bayerscher Schulbuch-Verlag

Sebeok, Thomas A. ed. 1960 Style in Language Cambridge: M.I.T. Press, and New York: Wiley

Stemmer, Nathan 1979 On the nature of meanings Semiotica 27.307-325

Wiener, Norbert 1954 The Human Use of Human Beings; Cybernetics and Society New York: Houghton Mifflin

Index of New Testament Passages